Pets and Crystal Therapy in harmony: Find the energy balance for your beloved furry companion

Author: Gonzalo Estrada

While every precaution has been taken in the preparation of this book, the publisher assumes no responsibility for errors or omissions, or for damages resulting from the use of the information contained herein.

PETS AND CRYSTAL THERAPY

First edition. March 14, 2024.

ISBN: 979-8224015719

Written by Gonzalo Estrada.

Table of Contents

Content

Chapter 1: Introduction to Crystal Therapy for Pets

When it comes to the well-being of our beloved furry companions, we may be willing to explore different holistic approaches to improve their quality of life. In this first half of the chapter, we invite you to delve into the fascinating world of crystal therapy and to discover how this ancient practice can benefit your beloved animal.

Crystal therapy is based on the belief that crystals and gemstones have energetic properties that can influence our body, mind and spirit. These gems contain different vibrations and, by using them properly, we can balance and harmonize our vital energy. But can crystal therapy also be beneficial for our pets?

The answer is yes. Like us, our furry companions are also made of energy and can sometimes have imbalances that affect their physical and emotional well-being. Crystal therapy can be a complementary tool to help them regain balance and promote their overall health.

Although our pets can't express themselves with words, it doesn't mean they aren't sensitive to the energies around us. Observing your partner's behavior can give you clues about how they're feeling and what areas of their life might need energy support. If you notice that your dog is anxious, for example, or that your cat seems irritable, crystal therapy may be a valuable option to consider.

So how can we apply crystal therapy for the benefit of our pets? The first thing to consider is the choice of the right stones. As with human beings, each animal has its own energy needs and preferences. What works for a cat may not work for a dog, and vice versa.

In this regard, it is important to learn about the energy properties of the different gems and how they can be related to the specific needs of your pet. For example, rose quartz is associated with love and calm, while amethyst is believed to help reduce anxiety and promote restful sleep.

Once you've selected the right stones, it's important to clean them and charge them with energy before using them with your pet. You can do this by running them under running water or leaving them in the sun for a while. These steps ensure that the stones are free of unwanted energies and ready for therapeutic use.

Then, you can place the stones in strategic places in your home, such as near your pet's bed or in their favorite spaces. You can also take a small stone with you when you walk together or even design a necklace with crystals specially selected for your companion.

Remember that crystal therapy is not a substitute for professional veterinary care, but it can complement it and provide additional support to your pet. It's always important to observe your companion and consult your veterinarian before starting any type of therapy.

In the second half of this chapter, we'll explore some specific techniques for using crystal therapy with our pets and how to integrate it harmoniously into their daily routine. Don't miss it! The healing energy of crystals could be a new path to well-being for your most faithful companion. In addition to choosing and preparing the right stones, there are different techniques you can use to apply crystal therapy for the benefit of your beloved pet. Next, we'll explore some of these techniques and how to integrate them harmoniously into your furry companion's daily routine.

One of the most popular techniques is placing stones in your pet's environment. You can create a small altar or special space dedicated to crystal therapy, where you can place the selected stones. This can be in your seating area, near your bed, or in a quiet corner of the house. Make sure that the stones are safe and that they do not pose a danger to ingestion for your pet.

Another option is to use stones in the form of a massage. You can hold the right stone in your hand and gently caress your pet with it. Physical contact combined with the energetic properties of the stone can help to calm and balance your companion. It's important to be attentive to your pet's reaction and adjust the pressure according to their preferences.

In addition, you can incorporate the stones in moments of relaxation and joint meditation. If you are in the habit of practicing yoga or meditation, invite your pet to join you in these activities, placing the appropriate stones near both. Not only will this practice strengthen the bond between you and your pet, it will also provide you with moments of shared peace and harmony.

You can also use the stones as a complement to massage therapy for your pet. As you apply gentle massaging movements to your body, you can hold a stone in your hand or even use it to make small circles in specific areas. This will help intensify the therapeutic effects of the massage and provide your partner with a moment of deep relaxation.

In addition to these techniques, it is important to remember that crystal therapy is a practice that requires patience and perseverance. Don't expect immediate results, as every pet is unique and may respond differently to therapy. Observe your partner and pay attention to any changes in their behavior, mood, or overall well-being.

Always remember to consult your veterinarian before starting any type of complementary therapy. They can guide you and give you specific recommendations regarding crystal therapy and your pet's particular needs.

In short, crystal therapy can be a valuable tool to promote energy balance and your pet's physical and emotional well-being. From placing stones in your environment, using them during massage or meditation sessions, to incorporating them as a complement to other therapies, there are many ways to integrate crystal therapy into the life of your beloved furry companion.

Don't hesitate to explore this fascinating world and discover the benefits it can bring to your pet! Together, they can find energy balance and further strengthen their special connection. Your beloved furry companion deserves the best, and crystal therapy could be a powerful tool to support him on his path to health and well-being.

Chapter 2: The Benefits of Crystal Therapy for Pets

Explore the many benefits that crystal therapy can provide to your pet and how it can help them find energy balance.

Pets are more than loyal companions; they are beings full of energy and sensitivity. As responsible caregivers, our main goal is to ensure that our furry friends are in an optimal state of well-being, both physically and emotionally. This is where crystal therapy can play a fundamental role.

Crystal therapy, an ancient practice based on the use of crystals, is known for its healing and energy strengthening properties. But what does this have to do with our beloved pets? Well, as living beings, our four-legged companions are also influenced by the energy that surrounds them. Just like us, they can face energy imbalances that can affect their overall health and well-being.

One of the most outstanding benefits of crystal therapy for pets is its ability to balance and harmonize their energy. The crystals work by emitting specific energetic vibrations that can help restore balance to our pets' bodies and minds. Each crystal has unique properties that can address different aspects of your well-being.

For example, rose quartz, known for its loving and calming energy, can be beneficial for anxious or fearful pets. This stone promotes relaxation and tranquility, helping to reduce the stress they may experience. In addition, rose quartz can also foster a deeper bond between you and your pet, thus strengthening your relationship.

Another crystal widely used in crystal therapy for pets is amethyst. This beautiful violet crystal has calming properties and can help relieve anxiety and improve sleep. If your pet is struggling to relax or suffers from insomnia, amethyst can be an ideal choice to provide a sense of peace and serenity.

Also, black tourmaline is a crystal to consider for pet owners looking to protect their companions from stress and negative external energies. Black tourmaline acts as a protective shield, absorbing and transforming negative energy into a more positive vibration. This can be especially beneficial for pets that are sensitive to or exposed to stressful environments.

In addition to balancing energy and promoting relaxation, crystal therapy can also help relieve physical ailments in our pets. For example, blue agate, with its anti-inflammatory properties, can be useful for those furry friends who suffer from joint or muscle discomfort. It can help reduce inflammation and promote healing in their bodies.

Every pet is unique, and so are their needs. It's essential to remember that crystal therapy is not a substitute for professional veterinary care, but can be a complementary practice to improve your overall well-being. It is always important to consult a veterinarian before introducing any type of alternative treatment.

In the next chapter, we will explore more deeply the different ways in which crystal therapy can be integrated into the daily lives of our pets, from the choice and placement of glass to specific application techniques.

So, get ready to discover how crystal therapy can help your beloved furry companion find the energy balance he deserves. Don't miss the second part of this exciting journey to your pet's well-being!

In addition to the benefits mentioned above, crystal therapy can also help our pets improve their concentration and focus. Have you ever noticed that your pet is easily distracted or has trouble keeping their attention on something? If so, you might consider using citrine. This bright yellow crystal is known for its ability to stimulate the mind and promote concentration. By keeping him close to your pet while he's training or doing activities that require attention, you can help him develop greater focus and better performance.

Another crystal that can be beneficial for our pets is carnelian, known for its motivating and stimulating energy. This orange crystal can be useful for animals that appear to be decayed or not energetic. By placing the carnelian near your pet, you can help it regain its vitality and enthusiasm, giving it a new spark of energy.

In addition to individual crystals, it is also possible to use combinations of crystals to take advantage of their complementary properties. For example, combining rose quartz with amethyst can help your pet find greater emotional balance, while promoting relaxation and tranquility. Similarly, a combination of black tourmaline and carnelian can offer even greater protection against negative energies and help boost your pet's energy level.

It's important to mention that crystal therapy can be used on a variety of pets, from dogs and cats to rabbits and birds. However, each animal may have different sensitivities and preferences. When introducing crystal therapy into your pet's life, it's important to observe their behavior and response to crystals. Some animals may show a greater affinity for certain crystals, while others may not be comfortable with certain colors or shapes. Always keep in close contact with your pet and watch for any signs of discomfort or rejection.

Remember that crystal therapy is not a substitute for professional veterinary care. It's always important to seek the guidance and advice of a veterinarian before using any type of alternative therapy with your pet. They will be able to provide you with the right guidance and ensure that your pet's health and well-being are not compromised.

In conclusion, crystal therapy is a complementary practice that can help our pets find energy balance and overall well-being. Whether it's to relieve stress, promote relaxation, improve concentration, or alleviate physical ailments, crystals can be powerful tools that allow us to provide love and care to our furry friends.

Don't miss the chance to explore this fascinating world and discover how crystal therapy can help your beloved furry companion find greater harmony in their life. Together, we can ensure that our pets receive the care and attention they deserve, so they can enjoy full and happy lives.

Keep reading and discover how you can integrate crystal therapy into your pet's daily life and continue to support them on their journey to energy balance!

Chapter 3: Types of glass suitable for pets

Pets are an integral part of our lives, providing us with love, companionship and joy. Like us, they have energies and emotions that need to be balanced to ensure their well-being. This is where crystal therapy can play an important role. In this chapter, we are going to explore the different types of crystals and stones that are safe and suitable for use on our beloved pets.

When it comes to choosing crystals for our pets, it's essential to consider their nature and individual needs. Every pet is unique and what may work for one may not be right for another. Therefore, it is essential to observe your pet and learn to identify what type of energy it needs to balance. By doing so, you'll be able to determine which crystals may be beneficial to her.

One of the most popular and versatile crystals for pets is rose quartz. Known for its gentle and loving energy, rose quartz can help calm anxiety and encourage relaxation in our pets. If you have a furry companion who is feeling restless or nervous, consider using rose quartz as a tool to promote a state of calm and well-being.

Another crystal that can be beneficial for our pets is amethyst. This beautiful violet-hued crystal is associated with wisdom and spirituality. Amethyst can help our pets balance their energies, promoting both physical and emotional harmony. If you notice that your pet is experiencing times of stress or imbalance, consider using amethyst to support their overall well-being.

Black tourmaline is another crystal that deserves special mention when it comes to pets. Known for its protective power and ability to absorb negative energies, black tourmaline can help our pets maintain a calm environment free of unwanted energy. If your pet seems to be affected by external factors, such as noise or environmental stress, consider using black tourmaline to protect it and keep it in an optimal energy balance.

Amazonite is another crystal that can be beneficial to our pets. Known for its balancing and calming energy, Amazonite can help relieve anxiety and fear in our beloved pets. If your furry companion shows signs of distress or is struggling to adapt to new situations, consider using amazonite as a support tool.

These are just a few examples of the many crystals and stones that can be suitable and safe for our pets. However, it's important to remember that every animal is unique and may respond differently to crystals. Observe your pet closely and pay attention to their behavior and reactions while using glass in their environment. This way, you can determine which crystals work best for her and how they can help her find an energy balance.

In the second half of this chapter, we'll explore more crystals and delve deeper into how to use them safely and effectively on our pets. We will discover how to clean and charge the crystals to maintain their optimal energy, as well as some specific techniques to apply them to our pets. Don't miss it! Read on in the next chapter to discover how you can make the most of crystal therapy for the well-being of your beloved furry companion. The second half of this chapter allows us to delve into more crystals and explore how to use them safely and effectively on our pets. Knowing the benefits of crystals we have presented before; we will now delve into other options that could be beneficial to our furry companions.

A very popular crystal among pet lovers is transparent quartz. This crystal has pure, balancing energy that can help our pets release any energy blockages and promote their overall well-being. If you notice that your pet is showing signs of imbalance or lack of vitality, consider using clear quartz to boost their natural energy and vitality.

Another crystal that can be useful for our pets is moonstone. This soft, luminous stone is associated with intuition and emotional connection. Moonstone can be especially beneficial for pets that have experienced emotional trauma or situations of abandonment. Using moonstone in the presence of your pet can help strengthen their confidence and promote a sense of security and protection.

If your pet has a physical condition, such as arthritis or inflammation, agate crystal may be an appropriate choice. Agate is known for its ability to relieve pain and promote physical healing. Using agate crystal on the affected area can help reduce inflammation and provide relief to your pet.

In addition to the crystals mentioned above, there are other stones and crystals that can complement the well-being and harmony of our pets. Carnelian crystal, for example, is known for its stimulating energy and can be beneficial for pets with low energy or in need of an extra boost. On the other hand, sodalite is a crystal that can help our pets to better communicate with us and strengthen the bond between human and pet.

As you enter the world of crystal therapy for pets, it's important to remember that every pet is unique and may respond differently to crystals. Watch your pet as you use the different crystals and pay attention to any changes in their behavior or energy. This will allow you to determine which crystals work best for her and how to use them most effectively.

Remember that safety is paramount when using glass on your pets. Make sure the lenses are placed securely and out of reach of your pet to avoid any risk of ingestion or injury. Always closely monitor your pet while using glass in their environment.

In conclusion, crystal therapy can be a wonderful tool to help our pets find an energy balance and promote their overall well-being. The crystals mentioned above are just a few options you can consider, but there are many other stones and crystals that may be suitable for your pets. Explore, experience and see the positive effects that crystal therapy can have on the life of your beloved furry companion.

I hope you enjoyed this chapter and are inspired to explore more about crystal therapy for pets. In the next chapter, we'll delve into how to clean and charge glass, as well as some specific techniques to apply them to our pets. Don't miss it! Read on to discover how you can make the most of crystal therapy for the well-being of your beloved furry companion.

Chapter 4: How to prepare and clean glass for your pet

L earn the proper techniques for preparing and cleaning glass before using it with your pet.

Crystals are wonderful allies in the energetic harmonization of our lives and, of course, in that of our adorable furry companions. If you are interested in giving your pet the energy balance it deserves, it is essential that you learn to properly prepare and clean the crystals before using them in their presence.

Just like us, crystals also accumulate energies and vibrate strongly. Therefore, it is essential to clean them of any previous energy load before starting to work with them. This process is done through purification, which consists of restoring its natural state free from previous influences.

There are several techniques you can use to purify your crystals. One of the most common is to immerse them in salt water for several hours, since salt has the ability to absorb and dissolve accumulated negative energies. However, be careful if you choose this method, as not all lenses tolerate prolonged contact with salt water. Some stones, such as selenite or tourmaline, can lose their luster or even decay, so it's important to research compatibility before using this technique.

Another effective way to purify crystals is through the smoke of incense or the burning of sacred herbs, such as Palo Santo or sage. These substances have the ability to cleanse and neutralize negative energies accumulated in minerals. Just pass the crystals through the smoke for a few minutes and see how the impurities are dissipated.

One technique that is especially appropriate for our pets is exposure to the sun and the moon. Light radiation and cosmic energy are powerful allies in the purification of crystals. Place your stones outdoors, preferably in a safe and secure place, and leave them exposed for a full day. Solar and lunar energy will be responsible for recharging and purifying your vibration.

Once you've purified your crystals, it's important to charge them with the right energy for use with your pet. You can do this process in a variety of ways, but the easiest technique is visualization and intent. Hold your glasses in your hands, close your eyes, and focus on love and connection with your beloved pet. Feel the energy flow from your heart to the crystals, imbuing them with the intention of harmony and well-being for your furry companion.

Remember that each crystal has a unique and special vibration that can help with different aspects of your pet's life, such as stress, health or protection. Therefore, it is essential to research and choose the right crystals to meet the specific needs of your beloved companion.

Dear reader, now that you have learned the proper techniques to prepare and clean the crystals before using them with your pet, you are one step closer to providing them with the energy balance they deserve. In the second part of this chapter, we'll explore in detail the different crystals and their beneficial properties for our adorable furry companions. I assure you that you will be amazed at everything that crystals can do for them! So, keep waiting and get ready to discover a world full of energy and harmony for your pet.

It will continue...

Now that you have learned the proper techniques to prepare and clean the crystals before using them with your pet, it's time to delve into the fascinating world of different crystals and their beneficial properties for our adorable furry companions.

Each crystal has a unique and special vibration that can positively influence different aspects of your pet's life, such as their emotional well-being, physical health and even their behavior. Next, I'll introduce you to some crystals that are especially recommended for your beloved furry companion:

1. Amethyst: This beautiful violet-hued crystal is known for its powerful calming and purifying energy. If your pet tends to be anxious or stressed, placing an amethyst near them will help them relax and find a state of inner peace.

2. Rose quartz: Rose quartz is the crystal of love and compassion. Its gentle vibration helps strengthen the bond between you and your pet, fostering mutual trust and providing a sense of security. In addition, this crystal can also promote emotional healing and harmony in the home.

3. Agate: Agate is a crystal known for its stability and balance. If your pet tends to be restless or nervous, carrying an agate with you or placing it on their bed is a great way to help them find serenity and peace of mind.

4. Carnelian: Carnelian is a crystal that stimulates vitality and motivation. If your pet has low energy or is apathetic, carrying a carnelian with you or placing it in its space can help it recover its vitality and enthusiasm.

5. Hematite: Hematite is known for its protective and rooting capacity. If you have a pet that is very sensitive to external energies or who easily feels unbalanced, wearing a hematite on their collar or placing it close to them will help them stay centered and protected.

These are just a few examples of the many crystals you can use to harmonize and balance your pet's energy. It's important to remember that every animal is unique, so it's advisable to research the different crystals and their specific properties before choosing those that are right for your companion.

Once you have chosen the crystals for your pet, it is essential to charge them correctly with the intention of harmony and well-being. You can do this process with a simple visualization and connection from the heart to the crystals. Feel connected to your pet and transmit your love and energy to the crystals, filling them with positive and beneficial vibrations.

Remember that using crystals as complementary tools is not a substitute for medical care or professional veterinary consultation. It's always important to have the support and supervision of an animal care expert.

Dear reader, I hope this second part of the chapter has expanded your knowledge on how to properly use crystals with your pet. Crystals are powerful allies in the well-being and harmony of our adorable furry companions. If you want to delve deeper into this fascinating world, I encourage you to research more about the different crystals and to explore their specific benefits for your beloved pets.

Don't miss out on the pleasure of sharing the energy and harmony of crystals with your life partner! Your pet will thank you with unconditional love and an even deeper connection between you. Continue to explore, experience and enjoy the wonderful adventure of pets and crystal therapy in harmony.

Until the next adventure full of positive energy and unconditional love!

Chapter 5: Crystal Therapy for Dogs: Improves Their Physical and Emotional Well-Being

Dogs are loyal and loving companions that bring joy and affection to our lives. As responsible owners, we're always looking for ways to improve their physical and emotional well-being. In this quest, we have discovered an ancient technique that can make a difference in the lives of our furry friends: crystal therapy.

Crystal therapy is a holistic practice that uses crystals and gemstones to balance and harmonize the energy of living beings, including dogs. These gems, with their unique vibration, can be a powerful healing tool both physically and emotionally.

Many may think that crystal therapy is simply a fad, but the truth is that this practice has ancient roots in different cultures around the world. Crystals have been used for centuries for their ability to balance and transform energy, and now we can apply their benefits to our beloved canine companions.

One of the highlights of crystal therapy for dogs is its ability to improve physical well-being. Each crystal has unique properties that can alleviate specific ailments. For example, amethyst is known for its calming properties and can help reduce anxiety and stress in dogs. Rose quartz, on the other hand, promotes emotional healing and can be useful for those dogs that have experienced trauma or loss.

In addition to these specific properties, crystal therapy can also strengthen dogs' immune systems, helping to prevent diseases and promoting their overall health. By balancing the body's energy, an environment conducive to physical well-being is created, increasing vitality and improving the quality of life of our faithful four-legged friends.

But crystal therapy isn't just limited to physical benefits. It can also be an effective tool to improve the emotional well-being of our dogs. Just like people, dogs can experience sadness, anxiety, or fear. Crystal therapy can help balance these emotions and promote calm and tranquility in them.

Each crystal emits a specific vibration that can affect dogs' energy field in a positive way. By placing crystals strategically around your environment or even on your necklace, you create an environment of harmony and balance that can help reduce stress levels and improve the mood of our furry companions.

Importantly, crystal therapy is not a magic solution or a replacement for veterinary care. We must always ensure that we provide our dogs with the necessary medical care and consult a veterinarian in the event of illness or injury. Crystal therapy is a complementary practice that can enhance the positive effects of traditional treatments.

In the next chapter, we'll explore in depth the different crystals and gemstones used in crystal therapy for dogs, as well as ways to apply them safely and effectively. You'll discover how to choose the right glass for your dog's specific needs and how to incorporate it harmoniously into their daily life.

Get ready to dive into a world of energy, balance and well-being for your faithful furry companion. Crystal therapy can be the key to improving your quality of life and strengthening the bond between you and your dog! Stay tuned for the second part of this chapter, where we'll delve into the properties of the most popular crystals and how to use them effectively. You'll find fascinating surprises that will push you to explore this wonderful practice! Dogs, as sensitive living beings, can greatly benefit from crystal therapy. In the first part of this chapter, we explored how this practice can improve your physical and emotional well-being. Now, in the second half of the chapter, we'll delve into the most popular crystals used in crystal therapy for dogs and how to use them effectively.

One of the best-known and most used crystals in crystal therapy for dogs is transparent quartz. This crystal has balancing and clarity properties, and can be beneficial for dogs that feel disoriented or have difficulty concentrating. You can place clear quartz near your resting space or even take it with you during walks to promote greater stability and focus on your dog.

Another popular crystal in crystal therapy for dogs is onyx. This crystal has protective and strengthening properties, and can be useful for dogs that have experienced trauma or are afraid. You can place an onyx on their necklace or near their bed to help allay fears and promote confidence in them.

Agate is another crystal that is commonly used in crystal therapy for dogs. This crystal has calming properties and can be especially beneficial for dogs suffering from separation anxiety. You can place an agate in their rest space or even take it with you when you leave them alone at home to help calm them down and reduce their anxiety.

In addition to these popular crystals, there are a wide variety of gems that can be used in crystal therapy for dogs. Depending on your dog's specific needs, you can choose crystals such as aventurine to promote heart healing and relaxation, or lapis lazuli to stimulate communication and strengthen the bond between you and your furry friend.

It's important to remember that dogs are individual beings with unique needs and preferences. When selecting crystals for your dog's crystal therapy, it's essential to pay attention to their behavior and reactions. See how it interacts with each crystal and if it shows a preference for a particular one. This will help you choose the most suitable crystals for your well-being.

Now that you know some of the most commonly used crystals in crystal therapy for dogs, it's time to learn how to apply them safely and effectively. It's important to note that crystals should never replace professional medical care or veterinary care. Crystal therapy should be used as a complementary practice to improve your dog's well-being and quality of life.

You can start by cleaning and charging your glasses before using them with your dog. This can be done using methods such as water, sunlight, or moonlight. Once the crystals are clean and charged, you can strategically place them around your dog's space or even on their collar. See how your dog reacts to glass and if he shows any positive changes in his mood or behavior.

Remember that every dog is unique and may respond differently to crystal therapy. Some dogs may show immediate changes, while others may need more time to adapt. Be patient and see the long-term effects on your dog.

In conclusion, crystal therapy can be a powerful tool to improve your dog's physical and emotional well-being. By using crystals strategically, you can provide them with a harmonious and balanced environment that promotes calm, tranquility and healing. Always remember to supplement crystal therapy with appropriate veterinary care and to be attentive to your dog's individual needs.

I hope you've enjoyed this exploration of crystal therapy for dogs and are excited to start applying it to your furry companion's life! Continue to learn about this fascinating practice and discover new ways to improve the life of your beloved dog. Have a trip full of energy, balance and well-being with your furry companion!

Chapter 6: Crystal therapy for cats: Harmony and balance for your feline

Explore how crystal therapy can bring harmony and balance to your cat, helping them to maintain good health and well-being.

Cats, with their elegance and mystery, have enthralled human beings for centuries. They are adorable pets and loyal companions that bring us joy and companionship in our lives. However, just like us, cats can face challenges and energy imbalances that affect their health and well-being. This is where crystal therapy can be a wonderful tool to restore harmony and promote positive balance in our beloved felines.

Crystal therapy is a discipline that uses the energies of crystals and gemstones to balance the body, mind and spirit. These crystals act as conductors and amplifiers of energetic vibrations, interacting with the cats' energy field and allowing for fluidity in their energy system. Some crystals that are especially beneficial for cats are:

1. Amethyst: This beautiful purple stone is known for its ability to relax and calm the nervous system. It can help cats relieve stress, anxiety and insomnia, giving them a sense of peace and tranquility.

2. Rose quartz: Rose quartz is renowned for its power to open the heart, promote compassion and emotional harmony. By having contact with this stone, cats can experience a sense of love and affection, which contributes to their emotional well-being.

3. Agate: Agate is a crystal that balances and stabilizes energy. It can strengthen vitality and improve the emotional connection between cats and their owners. In addition, it is believed that agate can help relieve joint and muscle pain in felines.

4. Amazonite: This green-hued stone is known for its ability to soothe and protect. It is believed to have purifying properties and can help cats eliminate energy blockages, thus improving their physical and emotional well-being.

It's important to remember that every cat is unique and may respond differently to crystal therapy. When introducing crystals into your feline's life, it's essential to observe any changes in their behavior, mood and overall well-being. Cats are highly sensitive to subtle energies and some may be more attracted to certain crystals than others.

To begin using crystal therapy on your cat, you can gently place the crystals in their environment. You can place them near their bed, in the place where they usually rest, or even take them with you during moments of interaction and shared affection. As you approach the cat with the crystals, pay attention to its reactions. If you show interest by touching or approaching crystals, you're likely reaping their energy benefits.

Remember that crystal therapy must be complemented by other veterinary care and wellness practices in your feline's life. Crystals are not a substitute for medical care, but they can add valuable support to help maintain energy balance and promote an optimal quality of life for your beloved furry companions.

As pet owners, our primary goal is to ensure the health and well-being of our beloved cats. Crystal therapy can be a unique and holistic tool to help our furry friends achieve a harmonious and balanced life. In the second part of this chapter, we'll explore how to select and use crystals more precisely to address different needs and challenges unique to our felines. We invite you to continue this fascinating adventure in the next segment of this chapter, where we will discover more about the benefits of crystal therapy for our beloved cats. See you soon! In the second part of this chapter, we will delve even deeper into the exciting world of crystal therapy for cats and explore how to select and use crystals more precisely to address different needs and challenges unique to our felines.

It's important to remember that every cat is unique and may have different energy needs. When choosing crystals for your feline, you need to look at their behavior, mood and general well-being to determine which are the most suitable for them.

If your cat tends to be shy or anxious, you can consider using the chrysocola. This beautiful green and blue stone is known for its calming and relaxing properties. By having contact with the chrysocola, your cat may experience a decrease in anxiety and a greater sense of calm and serenity. You can place the chrysocola near your bed or in your sleeping space to create a calm and safe environment.

On the other hand, if your cat shows aggression or dominant behavior, red jasper may be a beneficial option. This energy stone in reddish tones is known for its ability to balance and stabilize emotions. When in contact with red jasper, your cat may experience a decrease in aggressiveness and greater harmony in their behavior. You can carry red jasper with you during moments of interaction with your cat, to help promote calm and balance in their attitude.

If your cat has health problems, such as chronic pain or inflammation, opal can help relieve these ailments. This multicolored stone is known for its ability to strengthen the immune system and boost vitality in the body. You can place the opal near the place where your cat usually rests or even take it with you during moments of interaction and connection.

In addition to selecting the right lenses for your cat, it's important to use them properly. You can clean and charge your crystals before introducing them into your feline's life to ensure they are at their best energy. You can do this by immersing them in sea salt water for a few minutes and then exposing them to sunlight or moonlight for a period of time.

As you incorporate crystals into your cat's life, it's essential to observe any changes in their behavior, mood and overall well-being. Some cats may show a greater affinity for certain crystals and benefit more from their energy; however, each feline is different and may experience unique results.

Remember that crystal therapy should not replace traditional veterinary care, but it can be a complementary tool to promote your cat's health and well-being. Always consult a veterinarian before using crystal therapy as part of your feline's care.

In conclusion, crystal therapy can be a valuable tool to help our beloved cats achieve a harmonious and balanced life. By selecting and using crystals appropriately, we can work together with subtle energies to promote the health and well-being of our feline companions. Observe your cat, experience and discover the unique benefits that crystal therapy can provide.

We hope you enjoyed this fascinating journey into the world of crystal therapy for cats. In the next chapters of this book, we will explore different topics related to pets and crystal therapy in harmony. Don 't miss it!

Until next time!

Chapter 7: Crystal therapy for Birds: Promoting Their Vitality and Connection

The connection between pets and their owners is something very special. The relationship we build with our beloved furry companions brings responsibility, love and, above all, harmony. It's essential that we strive to understand and address the physical, emotional and energy needs of our beloved pets. In this chapter, we'll explore how crystal therapy can be a valuable tool to promote vitality and connection with our birds.

Birds, with their colorful plumage and their ability to fly, fill us with wonder and joy. They are sensitive beings and, like any other pet, they deserve to have a full and balanced life. Crystal therapy, an ancient holistic practice involving the use of crystals and gemstones, can help achieve that much-needed energy balance.

When we talk about crystal therapy for birds, it is important to remember that these winged beings have greater sensitivity and energy perception than human beings. Therefore, we must be especially careful when selecting the stones and crystals that we will use.

There are several crystals that can be beneficial to our birds, depending on their individual needs. One of them is rose quartz, known for its ability to promote unconditional love and harmony in the environment. Placing a small rose quartz crystal near your bird's cage can generate positive vibrations that promote connection and mutual trust.

Another highly recommended crystal in crystal therapy for birds is transparent quartz. This crystal has purifying and clarifying energy properties, helping to balance and stabilize the energy field of our birds. Placing transparent quartz in your bird's cage can help to create a calm and harmonious environment, promoting its vitality and well-being.

In addition to these crystals, there are others that can be of great help to our birds. Lapis lazuli, for example, is known for its calming properties and its ability to promote communication. If your bird shows signs of stress or tension, you can consider placing a small lapis lazuli near its cage, so that it can benefit from its harmonizing qualities.

Another crystal that is very useful in crystal therapy for birds is amethyst. This crystal offers relaxing and protective energy, promoting calm and emotional balance. By placing an amethyst near your bird's cage, you'll be creating a peaceful and serene space, helping it to maintain its vitality and connection with itself and its environment.

Now that we've explored some of the most recommended crystals in crystal therapy for birds, it's important to note that every bird is unique and may respond differently to different crystals. It's essential to observe your bird's behavior and reactions to determine which crystals provide the most benefits.

In the second part of this chapter, we will delve into the methods of applying crystal therapy to birds, as well as specific exercises and techniques to promote their vitality and connection. Read on and discover how you can use the powers of crystal therapy to further nourish and strengthen the bond with your beloved bird. You'll be amazed at the results you can get!

Remember, on this magical journey towards the integral well-being of your bird, crystal therapy can be a valuable tool to promote their vitality and connection. Don't miss the second part of this chapter, where we'll unveil techniques and exercises to strengthen the bond with your inseparable feather companion! As we mentioned earlier, crystal therapy can be a valuable tool to promote vitality and connection with our birds. In this second part of the chapter, we will delve into the methods of applying crystal therapy to birds and we will explore specific exercises and techniques to strengthen the bond with our beloved winged companion.

An effective way to use crystal therapy is through energy baths. To do this, you'll need some crystals of your choice and a bowl of clean water. Place the crystals carefully in the container and leave them in water for a few hours or overnight to recharge them with energy. Once the crystals are charged, remove them from the water and, very carefully, place the container near your bird's cage. The energy of the crystals will disperse into the environment, generating a positive effect on your bird.

Another technique you can use is crystal meditation. Before you begin, choose a crystal that is suitable for your bird and place it somewhere close to you. Sit in a quiet place next to your bird's cage and hold the chosen crystal in the palm of your hand. Close your eyes and take a few deep breaths, focusing on connecting with your beloved pet. Visualize a bright, warm light emanating from the glass and enveloping your bird, giving it peace of mind and vitality. Allow this energy to flow to your beloved bird as you focus on the connection and love your share. Stay in this meditation for a few minutes, and when you feel ready, gently open your eyes and watch your bird. You may notice a change in their behavior or a greater relaxation in their posture.

An additional technique you can try is the direct placement of the crystals in your bird's cage. Make sure you choose crystals that are safe for your bird and that don't pose a risk to its physical integrity. Placing the crystals near places where your bird spends the most time, such as their favorite perch or near their food and water, will allow them to benefit from the vibrational energy of the crystal throughout the day.

In addition to these exercises and techniques, it's essential that you always be attentive to your bird's needs and reactions. See if there are changes in their behavior, energy level, or mood after implementing crystal therapy. Each bird is unique and may respond differently to crystals. Remember, crystal therapy is not a substitute for proper veterinary care, but it can be used as a complement to promote your overall well-being.

In conclusion, crystal therapy is a powerful tool to promote vitality and connection with our beloved birds. Through the use of suitable crystals, energy baths, meditation and direct placement of crystals in the cage, we can help balance and harmonize the energy field of our birds, promoting their physical and emotional well-being. Don't forget to be attentive to your bird's individual needs and experiment with different crystals to find the most beneficial ones for it.

I hope that this second part of the chapter on crystal therapy for birds has provided you with useful and practical information to strengthen the connection with your inseparable winged companion. Remember that the relationship you share with your bird is unique and special, and crystal therapy can be a valuable tool in this magical journey towards the integral well-being of your beloved pet. Continue to explore and enjoy the benefits of crystal therapy in harmony with your pets!

Chapter 8: Crystal therapy for rodents: Well-being and serenity for your little companions

Rodents are wonderful pets that provide us with company and joy in our daily lives. These little beings have a unique ability to connect with us and can be an endless source of love and fun. However, just like us, rodents can also experience emotional and physical imbalances that affect their quality of life. This is where crystal therapy can play a fundamental role.

Crystal therapy is an ancient practice that uses crystals and gemstones to balance and harmonize our body's energy. Although it is best known for its application in humans, it can also benefit our beloved rodents. This alternative therapy uses the energy of crystals to stimulate the energy centers of the body of our little friends, helping them to achieve a state of well-being and serenity.

One of the most popular crystals used in rodent crystal therapy is amethyst. This beautiful purple stone is known for its calming and relaxing properties. By placing an amethyst near your rodent's cage, you are providing an environment conducive to tranquility and emotional balance. In addition, amethyst can help to dissipate stress and anxiety, relieving any tension your little companion may be experiencing.

Another stone that can be beneficial to rodents is aventurine. With its vibrant green color, aventurine promotes harmony and overall well-being. By placing this crystal close to your rodent's space, you're creating an environment in which their positive energy and emotional health can flourish. Aventurine can also boost vitality and growth, which is especially important for young rodents.

Rose quartz is another crystal that can be of great help to your rodents. With its delicate pink tone, rose quartz emits energies of love, affection and compassion. Placing a rose quartz stone in your rodent's cage can help foster a warm and loving environment, thus promoting a stronger relationship between the two. This stone can also help to calm any feelings of sadness or loneliness your rodent may experience.

In addition to these specific crystals, there are many other gemstones that can be beneficial to rodents. From the serenity of sodalite to the purifying energy of transparent quartz, each crystal has its own unique properties that can contribute to the well-being of your little furry companion.

It's important to remember that crystal therapy is not a replacement for proper veterinary care. You should always see an animal health professional if your rodent shows signs of illness or physical discomfort. Crystal therapy for rodents should be considered as a complement to veterinary care, helping to promote inner peace and emotional balance for your beloved friend.

In the second part of this chapter, we'll explore how to safely use crystals in rodent crystal therapy. We'll provide you with practical tips and step-by-step guides so you can effectively incorporate this alternative therapy into your rodent's life. Get ready to discover the power of crystal therapy and bring well-being and serenity to your little companions!

To be continued... In the second part of this chapter, we'll explore how to safely use crystals in rodent crystal therapy. We'll provide you with practical tips and step-by-step guides so you can effectively incorporate this alternative therapy into your rodent's life. Get ready to discover the power of crystal therapy and bring well-being and serenity to your little companions!

It's important to note that safety is paramount when using glass with your rodents. Make sure to choose stones that are not small or easy to swallow, as they could pose a health hazard to your rodent. You should also avoid any sharp-edged stones that could cause injury. It's recommended to use larger crystals that can be placed out of reach of your rodent, such as in an area close to their cage or where they spend most of their time.

An easy way to use crystal therapy with your rodents is to create an environment enriched with crystals specifically selected to promote their emotional well-being. You can place an amethyst, aventurine and rose quartz formation in the room where your rodent's cage is located. This will allow the energy of the crystals to spread throughout the space, creating a calming and balanced atmosphere for your little companion.

Another option is to place the crystals directly inside your rodent's cage, as long as they are large and safe enough. You can use a small platform or a corner of the cage where your rodent can interact with the glass safely. See how your rodent responds to different glass panes and adjust its placement according to your preferences. Some rodents may be attracted to and enjoy the company of the crystals, while others may show less interest. It's important to respect your rodent's individual preferences and provide them with options so they can choose how they interact with the crystals.

An interesting way to use crystals with your rodents is through guided meditation. If you have meditation experience, you can sit near your rodent's cage and gently guide a meditation while holding a crystal in your hands. The calming and balanced energy of the crystal can be transmitted to your rodent through the connection you establish during meditation. This can help create an environment of serenity and tranquility for your rodent.

Remember that every rodent is unique and may respond differently to crystal therapy. Watch your pet closely and keep in constant, open communication with them. If you notice that your rodent shows signs of discomfort or rejection towards the windows, remove them from their environment and look for other ways to promote their well-being.

In conclusion, crystal therapy can be an effective tool to provide well-being and serenity to your rodents. By choosing the right crystals and including them in your rodent's environment, you can contribute to improving their quality of life and promoting a healthy emotional balance. Always remember to consider safety when using lenses and, if in doubt, consult an animal health professional.

We hope this guide has been useful to you and motivates you to explore crystal therapy for the benefit of your little furry companions. Never underestimate the power of the energy of crystals and their ability to improve the lives of your rodents!

Chapter 9: Crystal Therapy for Exotic Animals: Balance and Calm for Your Unique Companions

Explore how crystal therapy can offer balance and calm to your exotic animals, promoting their energy balance.

Crystal therapy, also known as crystal therapy, is an ancient practice that uses the energetic properties of crystals and gems to harmonize and balance both the body and the mind. Although its most common use is in the human sphere, crystal therapy can also be beneficial for our furry companion friends, including those considered exotic animals.

Exotic animals, because of their unique and distinctive nature, require special attention to maintain their well-being and balance. Incorporating crystal therapy into their care can be a holistic and natural way to help these animals find that much-needed energy balance.

Like humans, exotic animals are also composed of energy, and the use of crystals can help to harmonize that energy, improving their physical and emotional health. Each crystal has specific properties and vibrations, so it's important to choose those that align with the individual needs of each animal.

Crystals can be used in a variety of ways in crystal therapy for exotic animals. A simple and effective way is to place glass in spaces where the animal spends most of its time, such as its terrarium, cage or play space. This allows the energetic vibrations of the crystals to permeate the environment and, in turn, positively affect the animal.

In addition to placing, it in the environment, another option is to use crystals in the form of jewelry or accessories that the animal can carry with it. For example, a necklace with a specific stone can help provide balance and calm to an exotic animal that may have high levels of stress or anxiety. It is important to remember that, as with any other type of therapy, crystal therapy should not replace adequate veterinary care, but rather complement it.

An exotic animal that can especially benefit from crystal therapy is the blue-tongued lizard, known for its colorful and fascinating appearance.

These lizards, native to Australia and Indonesia, can be dominant animals in terms of energy and require an appropriate balance to maintain their well-being.

Amethyst crystal is especially suitable for these lizards, as it helps to calm their energy and boost their balance. Placing a small amethyst crystal near the lizard's resting area can be beneficial to their overall peace of mind and well-being.

Another example of an exotic animal that can benefit from crystal therapy is the chameleon, known for its unique abilities to change color and adapt to its environment. Chameleons are sensitive animals and an abrupt change in their environment can cause them stress.

In this case, rose quartz may be a suitable option to help these reptiles find balance and calm. Placing small rose quartz stones in the chameleon's terrarium can help create a peaceful and harmonious environment, promoting their well-being.

As we have seen, crystal therapy can offer significant benefits to our exotic animals, helping them to achieve a state of balance and calm in their vital energy. However, it's important to remember that every animal is unique and may respond differently to crystals, so it's critical to observe and respect their individual reactions.

In the second half of this chapter, we'll further explore other stones and crystals beneficial to exotic animals, as well as some additional recommendations for their proper use. Get ready to discover how crystal therapy can improve the quality of life of your unique companions. Don't miss it!

Explore how crystal therapy can offer balance and calm to your exotic animals, promoting their energy balance. Crystal therapy, also known as crystal healing, is an ancient practice that uses the energetic properties of crystals and gems to harmonize and balance both body and mind. Although its most common use is in the human sphere, crystal therapy can also be beneficial for our furry companions, including those considered exotic animals.

Exotic animals, because of their unique and distinctive nature, require special attention to maintain their well-being and balance. Incorporating crystal therapy into their care can be a holistic and natural way to help these animals find that much needed energy balance.

Like humans, exotic animals are also composed of energy, and the use of crystals can help to harmonize that energy, improving their physical and emotional health. Each crystal has specific properties and vibrations, so it's important to choose those that align with the individual needs of each animal.

Crystals can be used in a variety of ways in crystal therapy for exotic animals. A simple and effective way is to place crystals in spaces where the animal spends most of its time, such as its terrarium, cage or play area. This allows the energetic vibrations of the crystals to permeate the environment and, in turn, positively affect the animal.

In addition to placing them in the environment, another option is to use crystals in the form of jewelry or accessories that the animal can wear. For example, a necklace with a specific stone can help provide balance and calm to an exotic animal that may experience high levels of stress or anxiety. It's important to remember that, like any other type of therapy, crystal therapy should not replace proper veterinary care, but rather complement it.

An exotic animal that can particularly benefit from crystal therapy is the blue-tongued squirrel, known for its colorful and fascinating appearance. These lizards, native to Australia and Indonesia, can be energetically dominant animals and require the right balance to maintain their well-being.

The amethyst crystal is especially suitable for these lizards, as it helps to calm their energy and improve their balance. Placing a small amethyst crystal near the scin's rest area can be beneficial to your overall peace of mind and well-being.

Another example of an exotic animal that can benefit from crystal therapy is the chameleon, known for its unique abilities to change color and adapt to its environment. Chameleons are sensitive animals, and a sudden change in their environment can cause them stress.

In this case, rose quartz may be a suitable option to help these reptiles find balance and calm. Placing small pieces of rose quartz in the chameleon's terrarium can contribute to creating a peaceful and harmonious environment, promoting their well-being.

As we have seen, crystal therapy can offer significant benefits to our exotic animals, helping them to achieve a state of balance and calm in their life force. However, it's important to remember that every animal is unique and may respond differently to crystals, so it's essential to observe and respect their individual reactions.

In the second half of this chapter, we'll further explore other stones and crystals beneficial to exotic animals, as well as some additional recommendations for their proper use. Get ready to discover how crystal therapy can improve the quality of life of your unique companions. Don't miss it!

In addition to blue-tongued lizards and chameleons, there are many other exotic animals that can benefit from crystal therapy. For example, snakes can be fascinating creatures, but they can also be prone to stress and anxiety. To help calm and balance these snakes, citrine crystal can be an excellent choice.

Citrine is known for its revitalizing energy and its ability to allay fear and insecurity. You can place small citrine crystals near or even inside the snake's habitat. In this way, the snake will be surrounded by positive energy vibrations that will promote a sense of calm and balance.

Another exotic animal that can benefit from crystal therapy is the scorpion. These arthropods may have intense energy and may be prone to aggression. To help calm a scorpion and promote energy balance, obsidian can be an excellent choice.

Obsidian is known for its ability to remove negative energy and promote protection. You can place small obsidian crystals near the scorpion's habitat, creating an environment of calm and security. You can also place an obsidian crystal in the scorpion's terrarium so that it is in direct contact with its energy.

In addition to these examples, there are a wide variety of exotic animals that can benefit from crystal therapy. For example, hedgehogs can be adorable animals, but they can also be prone to stress. To help soothe and balance a hedgehog, clear quartz can be an excellent choice.

Clear quartz is known for its ability to purify and strengthen energy. You can place small clear quartz crystals near the area where the hedgehog spends most of its time, thus promoting a sense of calm and balance.

The rat is another exotic animal that can benefit from crystal therapy. Although rats are commonly considered companion animals, they can also be very sensitive and prone to stress. To help calm and balance a rat, smoky quartz can be an excellent choice.

Smoky quartz is known for its ability to dissipate negative energy and promote calm and emotional stability. You can place small smoky quartz crystals near the area where the rat spends most of its time, thus creating an environment of calm and tranquility.

In short, crystal therapy can offer many benefits to exotic animals, helping them to achieve a state of balance and calm in their vital energy. Choosing the right crystals and placing them strategically can make a big difference in the lives of these unique animals.

However, it's important to remember that crystal therapy should not replace proper veterinary care. Always consult an animal health professional before implementing any type of therapy into your pet's routine.

In today's chapter, we've further explored other stones and crystals beneficial to exotic animals, as well as some additional recommendations for their proper use. I hope you found this information useful, and I encourage you to continue researching and discovering how crystal therapy can improve the quality of life of your furry companions.

Remember that your pets are very special beings and they deserve all the love and care you can give them. Crystal therapy can be a wonderful tool to complement your well-being and energy balance. Don't hesitate to try it and see the incredible results it can offer!

Chapter 10: How to Use Crystals with Your Pet

Learn different methods and techniques to effectively use crystals with your pet, depending on their specific needs.

When it comes to caring for our pets, we are always looking for natural and holistic ways to maintain their well-being and happiness. Crystal therapy has proven to be an effective tool for balancing energy and promoting healing in humans, but did you know that you can also apply it to your beloved furry companions? In this chapter, we'll explore how to use crystals with your pet, providing additional support for their physical and emotional well-being.

Before you begin, it's important to remember that every pet is unique, so it's crucial to adapt methods and techniques to the specific needs of your furry friend. Some pets can enjoy the presence of crystals while resting near them, while others may benefit more from using them directly on their body. Observe your pet's reactions and behaviors to determine which method is best for them.

An easy way to use the crystals is to place them around the space where your pet spends most of its time. Crystals such as rose quartz, lapis lazuli and amethyst are known for their ability to calm and balance energy. You can place them on your bed or in an area where your pet enjoys resting. As the crystal emits its subtle energy, your pet can absorb it and benefit from its healing properties.

Another technique is to use crystals as charms or necklaces for your pet. You can find necklaces specifically designed with natural crystals that fit snugly around your furry friend's neck. Some crystals, such as amazonite and agate, are believed to help balance emotions and promote harmony. By allowing your pet to wear a collar with these crystals, you can further enhance their emotional well-being.

If your pet is more receptive to direct contact with glass, you can opt for the technique of placing glass. To do this, select a glass suitable for your pet's needs and place it gently on their body. However, it's important to note that not all glass is safe for direct use on pets. Some crystals may be toxic or too hard for your sensitive skin. Be sure to do your research and consult an expert in crystal therapy before using any crystal directly on your pet.

In addition to these techniques, you can also use crystals to create a harmonious environment in your home. You can place them in different areas of the house where your pet spends time, such as their rest area, the place where they eat, or even in the garden. Crystals such as red jasper, green quartz and carnelian are commonly associated with protective and vitalizing properties. By keeping them present in your pet's environment, you can help promote their overall well-being.

Remember, using crystals with your pet is not a substitute for proper veterinary care. It's always important to follow the advice and treatments recommended by a professional veterinarian to ensure the health and well-being of your furry friend.

Keep reading and discover in the second part of this chapter how to combine crystal therapy with other techniques to give your pet an even more enriching and beneficial experience! Welcome back to this exploration of crystal therapy for pets! Let's continue to discover more techniques and benefits of using crystals with your beloved furry companion.

Another effective way to use crystals with your pet is through meditation. Like people, animals can also benefit from the relaxation and mental balance that meditation provides. You can create a quiet and relaxing space in your home to meditate with your pet and use the subtle energy of the crystals to deepen the experience.

To get started, select a suitable crystal for meditation, such as clear quartz or rock crystal. Place it in a visible place close to you and your pet during the meditation session. Sit in a comfortable position next to your furry friend and focus on the energy of the crystal. Take a deep breath and visualize how the crystal's energy expands and envelops both you and your pet.

As you immerse yourself in a state of calm and harmony, you may notice your pet relaxing and joining the meditation process. Notice any changes in her behavior or mood and use this moment to connect even more with her.

In addition to meditation, you can also use the crystals during play and exercise with your pet. Some crystals, such as sodalite or lapis lazuli, are associated with communication and expression, which can be especially beneficial during times of training or interaction with your furry friend.

You can place these crystals near the play area or take them with you during walks. The energy of crystals can help stimulate communication and strengthen the bond between you and your pet, allowing them to better understand each other and enjoy a richer gaming experience.

Always remember to observe your pet's reactions and behaviors when using the glasses. If you notice any discomfort or rejection, that particular crystal might not be right for her. Every pet is unique and may have different preferences, so it's important to adapt to their individual needs.

Last but not least, it's essential to keep your crystals clean and charged with positive energy. Just like us, crystals can also accumulate negative energies and need to be purified regularly. You can do this by submerging them in salt water for a few hours or exposing them to sunlight or moonlight for a few minutes.

In addition to cleaning, it's also important to recharge the crystals to keep their energy vibrant. You can do this by leaving them under sunlight or moonlight, or by placing them on a quartz druse for several hours.

By the end of this chapter, I hope you've discovered the beauty and benefits of using crystals with your pet. From relaxation and calm to communication and strengthening the bond, crystal therapy can be a powerful and harmonious tool for caring for your furry friend.

Always remember to consult an expert in crystal therapy or a veterinarian before using any glass directly on your pet, especially if you have any concerns or your pet has a health problem.

Thank you for joining us on this journey to the energy balance and well-being of our beloved pets! I hope you find inspiration and practical use of crystals in your daily life with your furry friend.

Chapter 11: Crystals for your pet's physical well-being

Our pets are loved and valuable people in our lives, so their physical well-being is critical to their happiness and quality of life. Just like us, human beings, our furry companions can benefit from the balanced and harmonious energy that crystals and stones can offer them. In this chapter, we'll discover what crystals and stones can help improve the physical well-being of our beloved pets.

One of the most commonly used crystals to promote the physical health of pets is rose quartz. Known for its loving and calming energy, this crystal can provide relief to our pets in times of stress, anxiety or illness. By placing a small rose quartz near your rest area, we can help calm your nervous system and boost your ability to self-regulate. In addition, this crystal is also believed to promote healing and strengthen the immune system of our pets, helping them to stay healthy and balanced.

Another crystal that can be beneficial to the physical well-being of our pets is amber. Known for its anti-inflammatory and analgesic properties, this crystal can help relieve pain and inflammation in our pets' bodies. Amber can be especially useful for animals that suffer from arthritis, joint pain or circulation problems. By wearing an amber collar, our pets can benefit from the healing properties of this crystal, reducing their discomfort and improving their mobility.

In addition, transparent quartz can also have a positive impact on the physical well-being of our pets. This crystal is known for its ability to amplify energy and promote clarity and vitality. By placing a small transparent quartz in the water our pets drink, we can energize and purify the liquid they ingest, providing them with a source of vitality and balance. In addition, transparent quartz can also be useful for relieving headaches and improving digestion for our pets.

One crystal that we cannot fail to mention is jade. This beautiful crystal is associated with health and well-being in many ancient cultures. For our pets, jade can be used to balance and strengthen the immune system, in addition to helping to alleviate skin problems such as irritations or allergies. By incorporating this crystal into our pets' daily care routine, we can help improve their physical well-being and promote healthy, glowing skin.

However, it is important to note that the use of crystals and stones for the physical well-being of our pets must complement adequate veterinary care. It is always advisable to consult with an animal health professional before implementing any type of complementary therapy. Our veterinarians are the experts in caring for our pets and can provide us with personalized guidance and recommendations based on the specific needs of each animal.

In the next chapter, we'll explore other crystals and stones that can benefit the physical well-being of our pets. We will discover how the right combination of energies can contribute to the balance and vitality of our furry companions. Get ready to dive into a world of harmony and well-being for your beloved companion! The physical well-being of our pets is of the utmost importance to ensure their happiness and quality of life. In this chapter, we have explored the benefits of some crystals and stones that can contribute to the energy balance and health of our beloved furry companions. But there are even more tools we can use to promote their physical well-being. Let's see what other crystals and stones can be beneficial to our pets.

One crystal that can make a difference in the physical well-being of our pets is black tourmaline. This crystal is known for its ability to protect and absorb negative energies. By placing a small piece of black tourmaline near our pet's rest area, we can help create a more harmonious and protected environment. In addition, this crystal is also believed to help balance the immune system, improving the resistance and resilience of our pets in the face of diseases or physical imbalances.

Another option that may be beneficial is Amazonite. This bluish green stone is considered to be a calming and balancing stone. Amazonite is believed to have anti-inflammatory properties and can help relieve muscle aches and discomforts related to the digestive system of our pets. By attaching an amazonite necklace or bracelet to our pet, we can provide relief and promote their physical well-being.

In addition, citrine is another crystal that can be beneficial to the physical well-being of our pets. This golden-yellow crystal is associated with vitality and positive energy. Citrine is believed to boost the digestive system and strengthen the immune system of our pets. By placing a small citrine in our pet's feeding area, we can boost their digestive system and promote better absorption of nutrients.

We can't forget about the amethyst crystal. This purple stone is considered to be one of the most protective and healing stones. Amethyst crystal is believed to help calm stress and anxiety, promoting a state of peace and balance. By using amethyst placed near our pet's rest area, we can contribute to improving their quality of sleep and emotional well-being, which in turn can have a positive impact on their physical well-being.

Finally, we will mention jasper. This stone is associated with balance and stability. Jasper is believed to help strengthen the circulatory system and promote the good health of our pets' internal organs. By placing jasper in the space where our pet spends most of its time, we can help to keep their energy balanced and improve their physical well-being.

Remember that, while these crystals and stones can be a complementary tool to promote the physical well-being of our pets, it is always essential to have adequate veterinary care. Consult your veterinarian before starting any type of therapy or treatment with crystals.

In short, crystals and stones can be powerful allies in the search for the physical well-being of our pets. From rose quartz to soothe and strengthen, to black tourmaline to protect and improve endurance, there are multiple options to benefit our beloved pets. Explore and experiment with these treasures of nature and see how balance and vitality are reflected in your furry companion. Take care of and love your pet with the magic of crystals!

Chapter 12: Crystals for your pet's emotional balance

Energy is a powerful force that permeates everything in the universe, and our pets are no exception. Just like us, our beloved furry companions can experience emotional ups and downs that can affect their overall well-being. That's why today we'll explore the properties of various crystals that can help balance your pet's emotions and promote their emotional well-being.

In the crystalline kingdom, there are several precious and semiprecious stones that are known for their properties to calm and balance emotional energies. By using these crystals properly, we can help our pets cope with stress, anxiety, and other emotional imbalances they may face.

One of the most powerful crystals to promote emotional stability in pets is amethyst. This beautiful purple stone is associated with tranquility and serenity, and its gentle energy can help calm nervous or anxious pets. Placing an amethyst in the area where your pet spends most of their time, such as their bed or favorite spot, can help create an environment of calm and relaxation.

If your pet tends to be hyperactive or has trouble staying calm in stressful situations, rose quartz can be a big help. Known for its loving and comforting energy, this crystal is perfect for balancing emotions and promoting a state of balance in your beloved animal. You can carry a small rose quartz with you on your pet's collar or harness, or place it near their rest area to help them stay calm during times of stress.

Another stone beneficial to the emotional balance of pets is lapis lazuli. This vibrant dark blue crystal is known for its stress-relieving properties and promoting communication and harmony. By helping your pets express their emotions in a healthy way, lapis lazuli gives them a sense of relief and emotional well-being. You can place a small lapis lazuli stone in their rest area or use it in a necklace specially designed for them.

In addition to these stones, there are many other crystals that can help promote emotional balance in pets. Turquoise, for example, is known for its ability to calm anxiety and promote confidence. Agate, on the other hand, can help pets overcome emotional trauma and find lost emotional stability. Finally, obsidian can be used to release negative energies and promote a greater emotional connection between you and your pet.

Remember that every pet is unique, and so are their emotional needs. It's always important to watch and listen to your pet to determine which crystals are best suited for them. As you explore the properties of these crystals and integrate them into your pet's life, you'll notice their emotional well-being strengthening and improving.

In the next chapter, we'll continue to explore more crystals that can help our pets find emotional balance and promote a life full of harmony and well-being. Get ready to discover more valuable tools that will allow you to care for and love your adorable furry companion even more. Continuing with the exploration of crystals for your pet's emotional balance, we delve into other precious and semiprecious stones that can help promote their emotional well-being and harmony.

Green quartz is an excellent choice for pets who can benefit from a boost in their emotional balance. This crystal is associated with heart healing and has the ability to release emotional blocks. If your pet has experienced traumatic situations in the past or if they have experienced significant changes that have affected their emotional state, green quartz can provide relief and support. You can place a small green quartz stone in your rest area or wear it in a special necklace to help balance your emotional energies.

Another crystal that can be beneficial to your pet's emotional well-being is carnelian. This bright orange stone is associated with vitality and confidence. If your pet tends to be shy or insecure, carnelian can help them reconnect with their inner strength and gain self-confidence. You can take a piece of carnelian with you on walks or outdoor activities to help your pet face new challenges with a greater sense of security.

Red jasper is another crystal that can be useful for stabilizing your pet's emotions. This reddish-hued crystal is associated with courage and inner strength. If your pet tends to be dominant or aggressive, red jasper can help you find a calmer and more peaceful balance. Place a small red jasper stone in your rest area or carry a necklace containing this crystal to facilitate your emotional stability.

In addition to these crystals, there are other options you can consider to help balance your pet's emotional energies. Aventurine is known for its ability to calm and balance emotions, especially in situations of stress or anxiety. Amber, on the other hand, is associated with vitality and joy, and can be useful for encouraging pets that are in a low mood. Citrine is a positive energy stone that can help increase your pet's confidence and optimism. Both aventurine, amber and citrine can be used in collars, harnesses or placed in your pet's rest area.

Remember that every pet is unique and may respond differently to different crystals. It's important to watch and pay attention to your pet's signals to determine which crystals are the most suitable for your pet. As you integrate these crystals into your pet's life, you'll notice their emotional well-being strengthening and improving.

With all this valuable knowledge about crystals for your pet's emotional balance, you'll be on your way to creating a harmonious environment and promoting their emotional well-being. Continue to explore and discover more tools that allow you to care for and love your adorable furry companion even more.

Remember that the next chapter will focus on other important aspects of your pet's emotional well-being.

Chapter 13: Crystals to Strengthen the Bond Between You and Your Pet

L earn how to use certain crystals and stones to strengthen the bond and connection between you and your pet. Living beings are integrated into an energy universe in constant motion, and our pets are no exception. Like us, they can also benefit from the powers of crystals and stones in their emotional and physical well-being.

In this first part of the chapter, we'll explore some recommended crystals to strengthen the bond with your beloved furry companion. Remember that every pet is unique, so you can experiment and adapt these recommendations to what you feel is best for your pet.

1. Amethyst: This crystal is known for its ability to balance energy and promote harmony. Placing an amethyst near your pet can create a calm and serene environment, helping to reduce anxiety and stress both for them and for you. It can also promote telepathic communication and strengthen the emotional connection between the two.

2. Rose quartz: Rose quartz is considered the stone of unconditional love. This crystal has the ability to open the heart and promote compassion and affection. Using it with your pet, it can help strengthen the bonds of love and affection between the two of you. In addition, rose quartz also has calming properties, which can be beneficial for nervous or scared animals.

3. Agate: Agates are stones that are characterized by their delicate appearance and variety of colors. These crystals have stabilizing and landing properties, so they can be useful for pets that feel unsafe or suffer from changes in their environment. The presence of an agate near your pet can help it feel protected and in harmony.

4. Tiger's Eye: This crystal is known for its ability to provide strength and positive energy. By using it with your pet, you can help increase their confidence and boost their self-esteem. In addition, the tiger's eye is a protective crystal, so it can help to ward off negative energies that may affect your beloved companion.

Remember that the choice of crystals to strengthen the bond with your pet depends as much on their needs as on yours. It's always important to listen to your pet and pay attention to their reactions and behaviors. See how you feel in the presence of the crystals and adjust the experience according to your preferences.

In the second part of this chapter, we'll explore practical ways to use crystals to strengthen the bond between you and your pet. You'll discover simple and effective techniques to incorporate the positive energy of crystals into your daily routine with your beloved four-legged companion. Get ready to be amazed at the possibilities that these powerful energy allies have to offer you.

Don't miss the second part of this chapter, where we'll delve into the fascinating world of crystals and their impact on the connection between you and your pet! Keep an eye out for the next few pages, where you'll discover how you can bring this wonderful harmony to your daily life with your adventure companion. In this second part of the chapter, I will introduce you to various techniques and practical suggestions for incorporating crystals and their positive energy into the daily routine with your beloved four-legged companion. These activities will allow you to further strengthen the bond and connection with your pet, creating an environment of harmony and well-being for both.

1. Joint meditation: Meditation is a powerful tool to connect with our own energy and that of our pet. Find a quiet and comfortable place where you can sit with your furry companion. Place the chosen crystals in front of both and close your eyes. Breathe deeply, feeling the energy of the crystals flowing through you and reaching your pet. Visualize an energetic cord that unites them, strengthening the bond and connection between them. Stay in this meditation for a few minutes, allowing yourself to enjoy this experience of tranquility and connection.

2. Crystal massage: Massage is a wonderful way to relax and bond with your pet. Select the right crystals for this purpose, such as amethyst or rose quartz, and place them on your hands during the massage. Focus on transmitting love, calm and positive energy to your beloved companion as you gently caress their body. The crystals will help intensify the experience, promoting your pet's physical and emotional well-being.

3. Crystal necklaces and leashes: Another way to incorporate the energy of crystals into your pet's daily life is to use necklaces or straps that contain specific stones. For example, you can choose a necklace with agates to help your pet feel protected and in harmony, or one with a tiger's eye to strengthen their confidence. Make sure you choose crystals that are safe for your pet and consult an expert if you have any questions.

4. Energetic spaces: Create specific spaces in your home where you can place the crystals to strengthen the bond with your pet. You can place small rose quartz or amethysts in your pet's bed, in the place where they eat or even in their play area. These crystals will help create a peaceful and harmonious environment, in which your companion will feel safe and loved.

5. Creative visualization: Creative visualization is a powerful technique that will allow you to connect mentally and emotionally with your pet. Sit in a quiet place and close your eyes. Imagine a bright,

warm light that envelops you and your pet. Visualize how this light intensifies and how small shiny crystals are released that adhere to your bodies, creating a deep and loving connection. Stay in this visualization for a few minutes, enjoying the feeling of togetherness and harmony with your beloved furry companion.

Remember that these are just a few suggestions and that every pet is unique. Always pay attention to your partner's reactions and behaviors and adapt activities according to their preferences and needs. Crystals are powerful energy tools that can help you strengthen your bond with your pet, but it's always important to listen to and respect your beloved companion.

I hope you enjoyed this second part of the chapter and that you find inspiration in these practices to strengthen your connection with your pet! Keep exploring the fascinating world of crystals and their impact on our daily lives. I wish you all the best on this journey of harmony and love with your furry companion!

Chapter 14: Crystal Therapy as Support for Pet Health Problems

L earn how crystal therapy can be used to support the treatment of different health problems in pets.

Our pets are a fundamental part of our lives, filling us with love, companionship and joy. As responsible owners, we always seek to provide them with the best and ensure their well-being at all times. Occasionally, our adorable furry companions may experience health issues that require specialized care. It is at these times that we are wondering if there are natural alternatives that can alleviate and promote your healing in a complementary way.

One of these natural alternatives is crystal therapy, a holistic therapy that uses crystals and semiprecious stones to balance energies in the body and promote healing. As in human beings, animals also have vital energy that can become unbalanced and manifest in the form of different physical and emotional conditions.

Crystal therapy has been used since ancient times to treat a wide variety of ailments in humans. However, in recent years, its use in the veterinary field has gained greater interest and recognition. Many pet owners have experienced the benefits of this non-invasive therapy on their beloved four-legged companions.

It is important to note that crystal therapy should not replace conventional medical treatment for pets. It is always recommended to see a veterinarian for a proper diagnosis and an appropriate treatment plan. However, crystal therapy can be used as a complement to promote general well-being and energy balance in our pets.

Each crystal and semi-precious stone has unique properties that can be beneficial for different pet health problems. For example, rose quartz is known for its ability to calm and reduce stress in animals. Their loving and gentle energy can help to soothe our pets in situations of anxiety or fear.

Red jasper, on the other hand, is renowned for promoting vitality and physical strength in animals. Their energetic and protective energy can be useful in pets recovering from illness or injury, giving them an extra boost in their healing process.

Another crystal widely used in crystal therapy for pets is amethyst. This crystal can have a calming and relaxing effect on animals, helping them to fall asleep and calm their minds. It's especially beneficial for those with stress or anxiety issues.

The way crystal therapy is used in pets can vary. Some owners choose to place the crystals directly on their pet's body, while others prefer to use necklaces or beds with inlaid crystals. You can also use the crystal elixir method, where water is prepared with the energy of the crystals and given to the pet.

It is important to be aware of the individual needs of each animal and to adapt the use of crystal therapy accordingly. Observing the response and well-being of our pets is essential to ensure that this complementary therapy is beneficial and does not cause any additional discomfort.

In the next chapter, we will further explore how crystal therapy can be applied to specific cases of pet diseases and health problems. We will analyze different case studies and share practical recommendations for those interested in experimenting with this therapy on their beloved furry companions.

Don't miss the second part of this chapter where you'll discover more about the incredible power of crystal therapy on the health of our pets! Continuation of the second half of the chapter:

In addition to the crystals mentioned above, there are many other options available in crystal therapy that can be used to support the health of our pets. For example, citrine is known for its ability to improve vitality and optimism, benefiting those animals that feel depressed or discouraged. Clear quartz is another crystal widely used in crystal therapy for pets, as it is believed to improve mental clarity and boost the immune system.

It is important to note that the choice of crystals and semiprecious stones must be done carefully and taking into account the particular needs of each pet. It is advisable to research the properties and benefits of each crystal to ensure that we use those that are most suitable for our pet's specific situation.

As for how to use the crystals, they can be placed directly on the pet's body for a few minutes a day, allowing the energy of the crystals to be transmitted through their skin. You can also use crystal necklaces or place them on your bed or in the room where you sleep. For those who prefer the crystal elixir method, water can be prepared using the energy of the crystals and given to the pet to drink.

It is important to remember that crystal therapy is a complementary holistic therapy and should not replace traditional medical treatment. It is always advisable to consult a veterinarian to obtain a proper diagnosis and an appropriate treatment plan for our pet.

In short, crystal therapy can be a natural and complementary way to support the health and well-being of our pets. Crystals and semiprecious stones have unique properties that can help balance the energies in the bodies of our beloved furry companions. However, it is important to be aware of the individual needs of each animal and to be attentive to their response and well-being when using this complementary therapy.

I hope this chapter has provided valuable information about the potential of crystal therapy in treating pet health problems. In the next chapter, we'll explore more specific case studies and share practical recommendations for those interested in experimenting with this therapy on their own pets.

Remember that our beloved furry companions deserve the best and we should always look for natural and holistic ways to promote their health and well-being. Crystal therapy can be a powerful tool on this path to energy balance and healing.

Don't miss the next part of this chapter, where you'll discover more about the impact of crystal therapy on real cases of diseases and health problems in pets!

Chapter 15: The Power of Crystal Therapy to Reduce Stress in Pets

Learn how certain crystals can help reduce stress and anxiety in your pets, promoting their overall well-being.

As pet owners, we're always looking for ways to ensure the happiness and well-being of our furry companions. It's important to remember that our beloved pets can also experience stress and anxiety in a variety of situations. Whether it's due to loud noises, changes in the environment, or even visits to the vet, stress can negatively affect the health of our adorable pets.

This is where crystal therapy can be of great help. This ancient practice uses crystals and stones to balance energy in the body and help heal different physical and emotional aspects. Just as crystal therapy benefits human beings, it can also be beneficial for our pets.

There are certain crystals that have specific properties that can help relieve stress in pets. Next, we'll explore some of these crystals and how they can be used to promote the well-being of your beloved furry companion.

One of the most commonly used crystals to reduce stress in pets is amethyst. This beautiful purple crystal has relaxing properties that can help calm anxious pets. Placing an amethyst in the space where your pet spends most of their time, such as their bed or near their rest area, can have a calming effect on them.

Another beneficial crystal for reducing stress in pets is aventurine. This soft green stone has calming and balancing properties. Placing an aventurine near the place where your pet relaxes, such as an outdoor space or next to their bed, can help reduce anxiety and promote a state of calm.

Rose quartz is also a crystal that can be beneficial to your pets. With its gentle energy of love and compassion, rose quartz can help relieve stress and foster a sense of security in your adorable furry companions. You can consider placing rose quartz in a place where your pet spends a lot of time, such as their play area or near their food bowl.

In addition to these crystals, there are many other options available to help reduce stress in pets. Amazonite, Labradorite and Lapis Lazuli are just a few examples of crystals that can be beneficial. It's important to remember that every pet is unique, so it can be useful to observe your furry friend's reaction and behavior when introducing a crystal into their environment.

By using these crystals as a complementary tool, you can help your pet find greater balance and reduce stress in their lives. However, it is essential to remember that crystal therapy should not replace proper veterinary care. Always consult an animal health professional for the best advice on your pet's well-being.

In the second part of this chapter, we'll explore how you can use these crystals effectively and how to incorporate crystal therapy into your pet's daily life. But before we continue, let's take a closer look at the importance of the emotional well-being of our adorable pets and how stress can negatively affect them.

To be continued... In the second part of this chapter, we'll dive deeper into how to use these crystals effectively and how to incorporate crystal therapy into your pet's daily life. But first, let's explore more closely the importance of the emotional well-being of our adorable pets and how stress can negatively affect them.

Our pets are more than just furry companions. They are sensitive beings with their own emotions and needs. Just like us, they can experience stress and anxiety in a variety of situations. This can manifest itself in different ways, such as destructive behavior, excessive barking, aggressiveness, or even physical health problems. It is essential that as pet owners, we are aware of the signs of stress and anxiety in our four-legged friends, so that we can intervene and help them find the necessary emotional balance.

Crystal therapy can be a valuable tool for reducing stress in pets and promoting their overall well-being. By using certain crystals with specific properties, we can create a harmonious and peaceful environment for our pets. Now, we'll explore how you can use crystals effectively.

A simple but effective way to use crystals is to place them in the space where your pet spends most of its time. You can create a small altar or special area near his bed, the place where he relaxes, or even in his play area. Place the crystals strategically so that they are visible and accessible to your pet. This will allow the stone's energy to flow to it and help reduce stress.

In addition to placing the crystals in your pet's environment, you can also consider taking them with you when using crystals for healing. For example, if you're doing a crystal meditation session, invite your pet to join you and place the crystals near it. This will allow them to absorb the healing vibrations and benefit from the calming effects of crystal therapy.

Another effective technique is to use crystal jewelry on your pet. You can purchase special necklaces or bracelets designed for pets that contain beneficial crystals such as amethyst, aventurine or rose quartz. These necklaces and bracelets can be worn as ornaments regularly and help keep your pet in a state of calm and balance.

Remember that every pet is unique and may have a different preference or response to crystals. Observe your pet's behavior and reaction when introducing crystals into their life. If you notice that they are showing greater calm, relaxation and well-being, it's an indication that crystal therapy is being effective for them.

However, it's important to note that crystal therapy should not replace proper veterinary care. Always consult an animal health professional to get the best advice about your pet's well-being and to address any stress or anxiety issues they may have.

In short, crystal therapy can be a powerful tool for reducing stress and promoting emotional well-being in our pets. Using crystals such as amethyst, aventurine and rose quartz, we can help create a harmonious and peaceful environment for our adorable furry companions. Whether it's placing the crystals in their environment, wearing them with you during crystal therapy sessions, or using crystal jewelry, there are multiple ways to incorporate crystal therapy into your pet's daily life.

Always remember to be attentive to your pet's needs and signs of stress, and look for additional ways to promote their physical and emotional well-being. Our pets give us so much love and companionship, they deserve the best care and support on their path to a balanced and happy life.

Chapter 16: Crystal therapy in moments of grief and farewell

Explore how crystal therapy can provide emotional support during times of grief and farewell to your pet.

Sometimes, our beloved furry companions reach a point in their lives where they must leave. It's one of the most difficult and painful situations pet owners can face. The special bond we have created with them over the years becomes even more intense when we realize that it's time to say goodbye.

The loss of a pet can trigger deep sadness and a period of grief. It's important to attend to our emotions and find healthy ways to go through this process. This is where crystal therapy can be of great help.

Natural crystals and stones have been used for centuries for their ability to balance and harmonize our energies. They are a powerful tool to support us emotionally and to help us heal.

When faced with the difficult task of saying goodbye to our pet, crystals can act as valuable emotional support. They can accompany us on our path to acceptance and inner peace during this grieving process.

One of the most recommended crystals at this time is rose quartz. Known as the crystal of unconditional love, rose quartz brings comfort and serenity in times of loss. Its gentle, calming energy helps to alleviate the sadness and emotional pain we experience.

Another beneficial crystal during grief is onyx. This black stone has a protective and stabilizing energy that helps us stay focused and grounded during turbulent times. It gives us emotional strength and resilience, which is of great value when we are dealing with the loss of our pet.

In addition to these crystals, there are many other options we can explore. Amethyst, for example, is known for its ability to promote emotional healing and relieve stress. Lapis lazuli, on the other hand, helps us to communicate with our deepest emotions and honor the grieving process.

It's essential to remember that every person has their own needs and preferences. The important thing is to choose the crystals that resonate with us and provide us with the emotional support we are looking for. You can experiment and explore different options until you find those crystals that give you serenity and comfort in your grieving and parting process.

Remember that crystal therapy does not replace the natural grieving process, but it can be a valuable tool to accompany us during this period. Crystals offer us a loving and protective energy that comforts us in the most difficult moments.

In the second half of this chapter, we'll explore specific crystal therapy techniques you can use to support you during your pet's grief and farewell. We'll discover how to use crystals effectively and learn to create a healing space to honor our furry companions.

Don't miss the chance to discover how crystal therapy can provide you with emotional relief in these times of pain and transition. Dive into the next part of this chapter and learn to connect with the healing essence of crystals. In the second half of this chapter, we'll delve into specific crystal therapy techniques that you can use to support you during your pet's grief and farewell. We'll discover how to use crystals effectively and learn to create a healing space to honor our furry companions.

A very useful crystal therapy technique during grief and farewell is crystal meditation. To get started, choose a crystal that transmits calm and serenity, such as rose quartz or amethyst, and sit in a quiet and comfortable place. Hold the glass in your hands and close your eyes to focus on your breathing.

Visualize your pet in a happy and peaceful place, where they are free from disease and pain. Imagine that you are surrounded by a loving and protective light, and allow that energy to envelop you. Breathe deeply and feel the healing energy of the crystal flow through you, providing you with comfort and emotional support.

During meditation, you can also place the crystals in different parts of your body to focus healing energy on specific areas. For example, you can place rose quartz over your heart to strengthen unconditional love and connection with your pet. Or you can place onyx in your root chakra, at the base of your spine, to keep you grounded and stable during this grieving process.

Another powerful technique is the creation of a crystal altar dedicated to your pet. Choose a special surface, such as a piece of furniture or a small table, and place a picture of your pet there and some objects that remind you of it, such as their favorite necklace or toy. Then, place the crystals that resonate with you around these objects. You can use rose quartz to convey love and comfort, onyx to provide emotional stability, and lapis lazuli to facilitate communication with your deepest emotions.

The crystal altar becomes a sacred place where you can honor your pet and connect with their loving energy. You can visit him whenever you need a moment of peace and remember the happy moments you shared together. Sit in front of your altar, hold the crystals in your hands and allow yourself to cry, remember and heal. Let the crystals strengthen you and help you find acceptance and inner peace.

In addition to meditating and creating a crystal altar, you can also use crystals in a practical way in your daily life. For example, carry a small crystal with you in your pocket or bag and touch it when you need a reminder of the healing energy it provides. You can use onyx to stay centered and grounded in times of stress, or use rose quartz to remind you of the unconditional love that will always exist between you and your pet.

In conclusion, crystal therapy can be a valuable tool during times of mourning and farewell to your pet. Crystals provide us with loving and protective energy that helps us to go through this process with acceptance and serenity. Explore different crystal therapy techniques, such as meditation and creating a crystal altar, and find those that best suit you. Allow yourself to connect with the healing essence of crystals and give yourself the time and space necessary to honor your beloved furry companion.

Remember that grief is an individual process and there is no right or wrong way to live it. Don't be afraid to seek support if you need it, whether it's through support groups, therapy, or simply by sharing your feelings with people you trust. Trust yourself and the transformative power of crystal therapy to find emotional balance and healing during difficult times in life.

Chapter 17: Crystals for Energy Balance in the Home

Discover how the use of crystals can contribute to the energy balance in your home, promoting the well-being of your pets.

Our homes are places full of energy, both positive and negative. Sometimes, harmony is disturbed and this can affect the well-being of our pets. Would you like to know how you can help restore and balance energy in your environment? Crystals can be a powerful tool to achieve this.

Crystals are natural objects formed over millions of years from minerals. Each crystal has its own unique properties and vibrations, which can influence the energy around us. By carefully choosing the crystals and placing them strategically in our home, we can promote an environment of peace and well-being for our beloved pets.

One of the most useful crystals for harmonizing energy in the home is transparent quartz. This crystal is known for its ability to amplify positive energy and to dissipate negative ones. Placing clear quartz in a central place in your home will help balance energy and create a more serene environment for your pets.

Another crystal that can be beneficial for energy balance in the home is amethyst. This purple stone is associated with tranquility and spiritual protection. Placing an amethyst near your pet's bed will help create a peaceful and relaxing resting space. In addition, amethyst is also known for its ability to help relieve stress and anxiety, which can be especially useful for sensitive pets or pets that have experienced traumatic situations.

If you have more than one pet in your home, it's important to promote harmony between them. In this case, you can use rose quartz, which is known for its ability to promote love, friendship and compassion. Place rose quartz in a strategic place in your home where your pets spend a lot of time together, such as the living room or garden. This will help them to strengthen their bonds and to maintain a harmonious relationship.

In addition to the crystals mentioned above, there are a wide variety of options you can explore to balance the energy in your home. Black tourmaline is known for its ability to absorb negative energy, while carnelian is considered an energizing crystal that provides vitality and motivation. Amazonite, on the other hand, promotes communication and understanding.

Remember that each crystal has its own characteristics and properties. Before choosing them, research and familiarize yourself with them to understand their benefits and how to use them properly. Crystals can act as supplements to improve the energy of your home and, consequently, the well-being of your pets.

In the second part of this chapter, we'll explore how to clean and energize crystals, as well as how to incorporate them into your pets' daily routine. Get ready to discover everything that these wonderful gifts of nature can do for the energy balance in your home. Don't miss it!

As we delve deeper into the world of crystal therapy and its influence on energy balance in the home, we find a wide range of crystals that can be beneficial to our pets. In addition to the crystals mentioned above, there are others that can also bring harmony and well-being to your furry companions.

Agate is a crystal that has been traditionally used to balance energies and promote emotional stability. Placing an agate in your pet's room can help calm their anxiety and provide them with a calm and peaceful environment. This stone is especially recommended for pets that tend to be nervous or restless.

Opal, on the other hand, is a crystal that can help our animals to open up emotionally and to connect more with us. This crystal stimulates trust and communication, which can be especially beneficial in situations where our pets feel insecure or distrustful. You can place an opal in a place where your pet spends a lot of time with you, such as the living room or your room, to strengthen your bond.

If your pet is going through a period of change or transition, jasper can be a great help. This crystal is associated with stability and calm, which can provide emotional support during periods of stress or adjustment. Placing jasper near the area where your pet eats or rests can contribute to their well-being and help them face changes more calmly.

Also, we can't forget to mention the sunstone. This crystal promotes vitality and good humor, helping our pets to maintain a positive and cheerful mood. Placing a sunstone in a sunny spot in your home, such as near a window, will allow them to absorb their beneficial energy and enjoy an environment full of vitality.

It's important to remember that every pet is unique and may have different energy needs. Observe your furry companion and pay attention to his behaviors and emotions to determine which crystal may be most beneficial to him. You can experiment with different crystals and see how your pet reacts to each of them. Remember that, like us, our animals also have the ability to sense and respond to subtle energies.

Now that you've discovered a variety of crystals that can contribute to energy balance in your home, it's important to learn how to clean and energize these powerful allies. Crystals absorb and retain energy, so they need to be cleaned regularly to maintain their effectiveness. You can do this by running them under running water, placing them in the sun or moonlight, or using incense or sage spray. The choice of method will depend on the glass and your personal preferences.

In addition, you can energize your crystals by programming them with the specific intention of harmonizing and balancing the energy in your home. Hold them in your hands and focus on the energy you want to create, visualizing how crystals emanate that energy throughout space. Repeat positive statements or mantras as you do this, infusing the desired energy into the crystals.

To incorporate the crystals into your pets' daily routine, you can hold them gently while you pet or play with them. You can also place them near their beds, on their toys or in their favorite spaces. See how your pet responds to the presence of the crystals and how their well-being is improved.

Using crystals in the home to establish energy balance and promote the well-being of our pets is a powerful tool that all animal lovers can take advantage of. As you explore and experiment with different crystals, you'll be amazed at the positive impact they can have on the lives of your furry companions. Dare to discover everything that these wonderful gifts of nature can do for the energy balance in your home! Start exploring this fascinating world and be enthralled by the magic that crystals can bring to your home and your beloved furry companions.

Chapter 18: Important Precautions and Recommendations for Crystal Therapy for Pets

Learn the essential precautions and recommendations for using crystal therapy safely and responsibly with your pets.

Crystal therapy is an ancient practice that uses crystals and semiprecious stones to balance our body's energy and promote emotional and physical healing. This therapy can also be applied to our beloved furry companions, helping to improve their overall well-being. However, when using crystal therapy in animals, it is crucial to consider some precautions and follow important recommendations.

The first thing to keep in mind is that every pet is unique and can react differently to crystals. It's essential to observe your pet's response while undergoing crystal therapy and to be alert for any signs of discomfort or discomfort. If you notice any negative changes in your behavior or physical appearance, stop the session immediately and see a veterinarian.

Before starting crystal therapy with your pet, it is essential to properly prepare the environment. Choose a quiet, distraction-free place where both of you can relax. Make sure you have all the necessary crystals within reach and be careful when handling them to prevent them from falling or breaking. Remember that some crystals may have sharp edges, so you should avoid your pet from biting or ingesting them.

Another important aspect to consider is choosing the right lenses for your pet. Each crystal has specific energetic properties and can benefit different emotional and physical aspects. However, not all glass is safe for pets. Some stones, such as malachite and tiger's eye, can be toxic if ingested. Research and consult an expert in crystal therapy to ensure that the crystals you use are safe for your pet.

It is essential to remember that crystal therapy is not a substitute for professional veterinary care. If your pet is sick or has a health problem, you should always go to a vet. Crystal therapy can be used as a therapeutic complement, but it should never be considered as the only form of treatment.

In addition, it's important to note that not all pets respond the same way to crystal therapy. Some animals may be more receptive and enjoy the experience, while others may be more uncomfortable or restless during sessions. Respect your pet's limits and don't force them to participate if they don't feel comfortable. If you notice your pet showing stress or anxiety, stop the session and provide emotional support.

Finally, remember to clean and charge the glasses properly before using them with your pet. Crystals can absorb negative energies and it's important to keep them clean and purified. You can carry out different cleaning methods, such as leaving them in the sun, burying them in sea salt or submerging them in salted water. The charge of the crystals is also important, you can do this by placing them under the light of the full moon or using Tibetan bowls.

In short, crystal therapy can be a wonderful tool to improve the well-being of our pets. However, it's vital to take precautions and follow important recommendations to ensure your safety and comfort. In the second part of this chapter, we'll explore specific ways of applying crystal therapy to pets and provide you with a step-by-step guide to starting to use it with your furry companion. Don't miss it! The second half of the chapter will focus on how to apply crystal therapy to pets and will offer a step-by-step guide so that pet owners can begin using it with their furry companions. We will explore the different forms of application, as well as the importance of creating a relaxing environment for therapy. Below is the second half of the chapter:

Once you've taken into account all the important precautions and recommendations, you're ready to start applying crystal therapy to your pet. There are several ways to do this, and it's important to choose the one that works best for you and your furry companion.

The first option is to place the crystals in the area where your pet spends the most time. For example, if your cat usually sleeps in a specific corner of the house, you can place some crystals there to benefit their emotional and physical well-being. Make sure the crystals are out of reach of your pet to prevent them from biting or ingesting them.

Another option is to use crystals in the form of a necklace or pendant. You can find necklaces specially designed for pets that contain crystals in their designs. Not only are these collars a safe way to bring crystal therapy to your pet, they can also be a beautiful accessory for them.

If you prefer a more direct form of application, you can gently hold the glass in your hand and pet your pet with it. Make sure your pet is relaxed and comfortable, and see how it responds to the crystal's energy. Some animals may be more receptive than others, but it's always important to respect your pet's limits and comfort.

During the application of crystal therapy, it is essential that you connect emotionally with your pet. You can talk to him softly and convey love and calm while using the crystals. This will help create a relaxing and trusting environment for both of you.

Remember that crystal therapy should be a pleasant experience for your pet, so it's important to be present and attentive to their needs. If you notice any signs of discomfort or stress, stop the session and provide emotional support to your pet. Your pet always comes first and you must respect their well-being and comfort at all times.

Once you've finished your crystal therapy session, be sure to properly clean and charge the crystals again. This will allow them to remove any accumulated negative energy.

Remember that crystal therapy is a therapeutic supplement and does not replace professional veterinary care. If your pet is sick or has a health problem, you should always seek help from a veterinarian.

In conclusion, crystal therapy can be a wonderful and effective tool to improve the well-being of our pets. However, it is crucial to take precautions into account, respect the limits and comfort of our pet, and always seek the advice of experts in crystal therapy and veterinarians.

I hope this guide has provided you with the information you need to start using crystal therapy safely and responsibly with your beloved furry companion. Enjoy exploring this fascinating ancient practice and promote energy balance in your pet's life!

These lizards, native to Australia and Indonesia, can be dominant animals in terms of energy and require an appropriate balance to maintain their well-being.

Amethyst crystal is especially suitable for these lizards, as it helps to calm their energy and boost their balance. Placing a small amethyst crystal near the lizard's resting area can be beneficial to their overall peace of mind and well-being.

Another example of an exotic animal that can benefit from crystal therapy is the chameleon, known for its unique abilities to change color and adapt to its environment. Chameleons are sensitive animals and an abrupt change in their environment can cause them stress.

In this case, rose quartz may be a suitable option to help these reptiles find balance and calm. Placing small rose quartz stones in the chameleon's terrarium can help create a peaceful and harmonious environment, promoting their well-being.

As we have seen, crystal therapy can offer significant benefits to our exotic animals, helping them to achieve a state of balance and calm in their vital energy. However, it's important to remember that every animal is unique and may respond differently to crystals, so it's critical to observe and respect their individual reactions.

In the second half of this chapter, we'll further explore other stones and crystals beneficial to exotic animals, as well as some additional recommendations for their proper use. Get ready to discover how crystal therapy can improve the quality of life of your unique companions. Don't miss it!

Explore how crystal therapy can offer balance and calm to your exotic animals, promoting their energy balance. Crystal therapy, also known as crystal healing, is an ancient practice that uses the energetic properties of crystals and gems to harmonize and balance both body and mind. Although its most common use is in the human sphere, crystal therapy can also be beneficial for our furry companions, including those considered exotic animals.

Exotic animals, because of their unique and distinctive nature, require special attention to maintain their well-being and balance. Incorporating crystal therapy into their care can be a holistic and natural way to help these animals find that much needed energy balance.

Like humans, exotic animals are also composed of energy, and the use of crystals can help to harmonize that energy, improving their physical and emotional health. Each crystal has specific properties and vibrations, so it's important to choose those that align with the individual needs of each animal.

Crystals can be used in a variety of ways in crystal therapy for exotic animals. A simple and effective way is to place crystals in spaces where the animal spends most of its time, such as its terrarium, cage or play area. This allows the energetic vibrations of the crystals to permeate the environment and, in turn, positively affect the animal.

In addition to placing them in the environment, another option is to use crystals in the form of jewelry or accessories that the animal can wear. For example, a necklace with a specific stone can help provide balance and calm to an exotic animal that may experience high levels of stress or anxiety. It's important to remember that, like any other type of therapy, crystal therapy should not replace proper veterinary care, but rather complement it.

An exotic animal that can particularly benefit from crystal therapy is the blue-tongued squirrel, known for its colorful and fascinating appearance. These lizards, native to Australia and Indonesia, can be energetically dominant animals and require the right balance to maintain their well-being.

The amethyst crystal is especially suitable for these lizards, as it helps to calm their energy and improve their balance. Placing a small amethyst crystal near the skin's rest area can be beneficial to your overall peace of mind and well-being.

Another example of an exotic animal that can benefit from crystal therapy is the chameleon, known for its unique abilities to change color and adapt to its environment. Chameleons are sensitive animals, and a sudden change in their environment can cause them stress.

In this case, rose quartz may be a suitable option to help these reptiles find balance and calm. Placing small pieces of rose quartz in the chameleon's terrarium can contribute to creating a peaceful and harmonious environment, promoting their well-being.

As we have seen, crystal therapy can offer significant benefits to our exotic animals, helping them to achieve a state of balance and calm in their life force. However, it's important to remember that every animal is unique and may respond differently to crystals, so it's essential to observe and respect their individual reactions.

In the second half of this chapter, we'll further explore other stones and crystals beneficial to exotic animals, as well as some additional recommendations for their proper use. Get ready to discover how crystal therapy can improve the quality of life of your unique companions. Don't miss it!

In addition to blue-tongued lizards and chameleons, there are many other exotic animals that can benefit from crystal therapy. For example, snakes can be fascinating creatures, but they can also be prone to stress and anxiety. To help calm and balance these snakes, citrine crystal can be an excellent choice.

Citrine is known for its revitalizing energy and its ability to allay fear and insecurity. You can place small citrine crystals near or even inside the snake's habitat. In this way, the snake will be surrounded by positive energy vibrations that will promote a sense of calm and balance.

Another exotic animal that can benefit from crystal therapy is the scorpion. These arthropods may have intense energy and may be prone to aggression. To help calm a scorpion and promote energy balance, obsidian can be an excellent choice.

Obsidian is known for its ability to remove negative energy and promote protection. You can place small obsidian crystals near the scorpion's habitat, creating an environment of calm and security. You can also place an obsidian crystal in the scorpion's terrarium so that it is in direct contact with its energy.

In addition to these examples, there are a wide variety of exotic animals that can benefit from crystal therapy. For example, hedgehogs can be adorable animals, but they can also be prone to stress. To help soothe and balance a hedgehog, clear quartz can be an excellent choice.

Clear quartz is known for its ability to purify and strengthen energy. You can place small clear quartz crystals near the area where the hedgehog spends most of its time, thus promoting a sense of calm and balance.

The rat is another exotic animal that can benefit from crystal therapy. Although rats are commonly considered companion animals, they can also be very sensitive and prone to stress. To help calm and balance a rat, smoky quartz can be an excellent choice.

Smoky quartz is known for its ability to dissipate negative energy and promote calm and emotional stability. You can place small smoky quartz crystals near the area where the rat spends most of its time, thus creating an environment of calm and tranquility.

In short, crystal therapy can offer many benefits to exotic animals, helping them to achieve a state of balance and calm in their vital energy. Choosing the right crystals and placing them strategically can make a big difference in the lives of these unique animals.

However, it's important to remember that crystal therapy should not replace proper veterinary care. Always consult an animal health professional before implementing any type of therapy into your pet's routine.

In today's chapter, we've further explored other stones and crystals beneficial to exotic animals, as well as some additional recommendations for their proper use. I hope you found this information useful, and I encourage you to continue researching and discovering how crystal therapy can improve the quality of life of your furry companions.

Remember that your pets are very special beings and they deserve all the love and care you can give them. Crystal therapy can be a wonderful tool to complement your well-being and energy balance. Don't hesitate to try it and see the incredible results it can offer!

Chapter 19: Success Stories: Real Testimonials About Pet Crystal Therapy

Learn real stories of people who have experienced the benefits of crystal therapy on their pets and how it has transformed their lives.

Crystal therapy, an ancient practice that uses crystals and semiprecious stones to improve physical, mental and emotional well-being, is not only beneficial for human beings, but also for our adorable pets. In this chapter, we will share with you real testimonies that show how crystal therapy has positively impacted the lives of owners and their furry companions.

Our first success story stars Luna, a mischievous mixed-breed dog. Marina, her owner, noticed that Luna was restless and anxious during storms, making it difficult for her to relax and rest. After researching natural alternatives, Marina decided to try crystal therapy. He introduced a beautiful amethyst stone, known for its calming and balancing properties, into the Luna necklace. To her surprise, Luna began to show a significant reduction in her anxiety during storms. Now, Marina and Luna enjoy moments of tranquility and serenity in every rain.

Our next testimonial highlights the positive impact of crystal therapy on a cat named Simon. Andrés, his owner, noticed that Simon had difficulty falling asleep and often woke up during the night.

Concerned about his well-being, Andrés sought a natural solution and discovered that rose quartz stone was known to promote calm and relaxation. Andrew placed a small stone under Simon's bed, near his sleeping area. Over time, Simon began to sleep peacefully throughout the night, waking up more rested and fuller of energy to enjoy the day.

In our third story, we meet Lucas, José's companion dog. Lucas used to experience muscle pain and stiffness due to his arthritis, affecting his mobility and quality of life. José, looking for complementary alternatives to traditional medical treatments, discovered the benefits of crystal therapy to alleviate pain and promote flexibility. He purchased an amber stone, known for its anti-inflammatory and comforting properties, and placed it near Lucas' rest area. Over time, Lucas experienced a marked improvement in his mobility and a significant reduction in pain, allowing him to enjoy activities and walks again.

Each success story in pet crystal therapy is unique and personal. These testimonies show us how this ancient practice can have transformative effects on the lives of our beloved pets and their owners. Crystal therapy is not only a natural alternative, but also a way to connect with our furry companions through energy and harmony.

As we continue to explore more success stories in the second half of this chapter, get ready to discover how crystal therapy has influenced the lives of other pet owners and how it has strengthened their bond with their adorable companions. We can't wait to share with you the experiences and benefits that have come from this wonderful practice.

Remember, crystal therapy has the power to heal and balance both people and animals. Read on and dive into these inspiring stories that show how our pets can find the energy balance they so desperately need. In the second half of this chapter, we'll continue to explore more success stories that demonstrate the benefits of crystal therapy for pets. These stories show us how this ancient practice has strengthened the bond between owners and their adorable furry companions, as well as the positive impact it has had on their overall well-being.

In our fourth story, we will meet Mía, a curious kitten who used to be afraid and anxious about being alone at home. Her owner, Laura, was concerned about her emotional well-being and decided to try crystal therapy as a natural way to help Mia feel calmer and safer. After doing some research, Laura chose the transparent quartz stone, known for its ability to balance and harmonize energies. She placed the stone near Mia's favorite resting place and, over time, noticed that Mia felt more relaxed and confident, even when she was home alone. Now, Mia enjoys her time alone and has developed greater self-esteem.

In the following success story, we will meet Max, a Labrador Retriever dog who suffered from chronic digestive problems. His owner, Carolina, was desperate to find a solution that would alleviate Max's discomfort and improve his quality of life. After researching different options, Carolina decided to try crystal therapy and chose jade stone, known for its healing and balancing properties. He placed the stone near Max's bed and noticed a marked improvement in his digestion. Max stopped having the stomach problems that afflicted him and now enjoys a healthy and discomfort-free digestion.

In our last success story, we'll meet Beto, a songbird with behavioral problems. His owner, Elena, noticed that Beto was agitated and anxious, affecting his singing and his general well-being. After reading about crystal therapy, Elena decided to try an amazonite stone, known for its ability to calm and balance energies. He placed the stone near Beto's cage and, to his surprise, noticed a significant improvement in his singing and a decrease in his level of anxiety. Now, Beto sings with joy and feels calmer and more in harmony.

These success stories are just a few examples of how crystal therapy has positively impacted the lives of pets and their owners. The energetic connection and harmony that can be achieved through this ancient practice are truly transformative. Each testimony is unique and shows us how crystal therapy can help our pets find the energy balance they so need to live a full and happy life.

As we dive into these inspiring stories, I invite all pet owners to consider crystal therapy as a natural option to improve the well-being and quality of life of their adorable companions. The connection and love we share with our pets is priceless, and crystal therapy can be a powerful tool to strengthen that bond and improve the physical, mental and emotional health of our dear furry friends.

Remember, crystal therapy has the potential to transform lives, both for people and animals. If you're looking for a natural alternative to help your pet, consider exploring the wonderful practice of crystal therapy and discover how it can bring balance and well-being to your beloved furry companion.

In the following pages, we will continue to share more testimonies and moving experiences about crystal therapy in pets. Get ready to be moved and amazed at the stories of transformation and healing that have emerged from this beautiful practice. We can't wait to share with you more inspiring and positive stories about how crystal therapy has changed the lives of so many pets and their owners!

Chapter 20:
Implementing Crystal
Therapy in Everyday Life
with Your Pet

Crystal therapy has proven to be a powerful tool for finding energy balance both in our lives and in that of our beloved pets. While we have immersed ourselves in the world of crystals and their health benefits in previous chapters, in this chapter we will focus on how we can practically and effectively implement crystal therapy in our daily lives together with our beloved furry companions.

It is essential to keep in mind that our pets are sensitive beings and receptive to the energy that surrounds them. Therefore, as we begin to use crystals in their presence, we must be aware of their well-being and emotional state. Before proceeding, let's make sure that our furry companions feel comfortable and relaxed. If we notice any signs of discomfort or stress, it's important to stop the process and seek another form of energy balance.

A first step in implementing crystal therapy in daily life with our pets is to select the right crystals. Each crystal has unique properties and different energy vibrations. When choosing a crystal, we must take into account the specific needs of our pet. For example, if our pet tends to be anxious or nervous, we could opt for crystals such as amethyst, amazonite or rose quartz, which help calm the mind and promote relaxation.

Once we have selected the right crystals, we can incorporate them into different aspects of daily life with our pet. For example, we can place them on your bed or in your favorite sleeping area, so that crystal energy is present during your moments of relaxation and sleep. We can also take our pet for a walk with a collar or strap that contains crystals, thus allowing them to be in direct contact with their healing energy.

Another practical way to incorporate crystal therapy into everyday life with our pets is through meditation and joint relaxation sessions. We can create a calm and harmonious space in our house, where we can sit next to our pet and hold the crystals in our hands. As we immerse ourselves in a state of serenity, we can visualize the healing energy of crystals flowing both in us and in our pet. This energetic connection will strengthen the bond between the two and promote a sense of mutual well-being.

Let's not forget that crystal therapy also invites us to connect with nature. If we have the opportunity, we can take our pet to places where there is a natural presence of crystals, such as a beach with quartz sand or a crystal forest. These natural environments enhanced the healing energy of the crystals and will provide our pet with an enriching experience.

In short, by integrating crystal therapy in a practical and effective way into our daily lives together with our pet, we are providing an opportunity to increase their physical, emotional and spiritual well-being. By choosing the right crystals and allowing their energy to flow in their environment, we are opening doors to a deep and harmonious energy balance. Interacting with crystals can be a fascinating and enriching experience for both us and our beloved pets.

In the second part of this chapter, we will discover practical exercises and additional tips that will help us to go even deeper into the implementation of crystal therapy in everyday life. Don't miss out and continue exploring this fascinating path to energy balance with us with your furry companion! In this second part of the chapter, we will continue to explore various ways to implement crystal therapy in everyday life with our pets. Continuing our intention to promote the physical, emotional and spiritual well-being of our beloved furry companions, we will discover more practical exercises and additional tips.

A practical exercise that we can do is placing glass around the house. We can strategically distribute different types of crystals in areas where our pets spend more time, such as their play area or rest area. For example, fluorite can promote concentration and focus, so it would be ideal to place it near your bed or play corner. Sodalite, on the other hand, encourages communication and harmony, so it can be beneficial in shared spaces. Around your food plate, we can place a bowl with quartz stones to enhance the vital energy of the food you eat. These small additions to our environment can make a big difference in our pets' energy balance.

In addition to the strategic placement of crystals, we can complement crystal therapy with other practices such as aromatherapy. Some natural essences, such as lavender essential oil, can perfectly complement the benefits of crystals. We can apply a small amount of lavender oil to our hands and then gently pet our pet. As our furry companions inhale the relaxing scent of lavender, the combination with the healing energy of the crystals can intensify their experience of relaxation and well-being.

Another valuable tip is the use of crystals during moments of play and training. We can find toys designed specifically for pets that contain embedded crystals or wrapped in durable mesh. These toys can help stimulate both the mind and body of our pets, while providing them with the energy benefits of crystals. By interacting with these toys, our pets are also receiving a crystal therapy session without even realizing it.

In addition to toys, we can use crystals in clicker training sessions. By carrying a crystal in our pocket during the session, we can take advantage of its energy to promote our pet's concentration and attention. Crystals such as scolecite or tiger's eye can be especially beneficial for this purpose. As we practice training, the energy connection between us and our pets is strengthened, thus facilitating communication and learning.

Last but not least, it's essential to remember that we are an example for our pets. Our attitude, emotional state and energy also influence them. Therefore, it is important to cultivate our own practice of crystal therapy and energy balance. If we feel balanced and in harmony, our pets are more likely to experience that state of well-being as well. Therefore, let's take time to connect with our crystals, perform meditations, or practice relaxation techniques. By cultivating our own energy, we are providing an optimal environment for our pets to fully benefit from crystal therapy.

In conclusion, crystal therapy is a powerful tool that can transform the lives of our pets. By implementing it in a practical and effective way in our daily lives, we provide our pets with the opportunity to experience a deep and harmonious energy balance. Whether it's placing crystals strategically, combining them with aromatherapy, using crystals during play and training, or cultivating our own energy balancing practice, we are creating a space in which our pets can flourish and thrive. Continue to explore and enjoy the wonderful world of crystal therapy with your beloved furry companion!

Disclaimer

This eBook is provided for informational and educational purposes only. It is not intended as a substitute for professional advice, diagnosis or treatment. The opinions and contents presented in this book are those of the author and should not be interpreted as advice specific to your particular situation.

While considerable effort has been made to ensure that the information provided in this eBook is accurate and useful, the author and publishers cannot guarantee the accuracy, appropriateness or completeness of any information and will not be responsible for errors, omissions or results obtained from the use of such information.

Readers are advised to consult qualified professionals in the relevant fields before making any decision based on the content of this eBook. Use or reliance on any information contained in this book is at your own risk.

The author and publishers of this eBook specifically disclaim any liability, loss or risk, personal or otherwise, incurred as a result, directly or indirectly, of the use and application of any content in this eBook.

Don't miss out!

Visit the website below and you can sign up to receive emails whenever Gonzalo Estrada publishes a new book. There's no charge and no obligation.

https://books2read.com/r/B-A-OZBBB-CMJZC

BOOKS 2 READ

Connecting independent readers to independent writers.

Did you love *Pets and Crystal Therapy*? Then you should read *Aromatherapy, The natural path to your pet´s well being*[1] by Gonzalo Estrada!

[2]

Aromatherapy: The Natural Path to Your Pet's Well-being" by Gonzalo Estrada is a comprehensive guide that introduces pet owners to the gentle art of aromatherapy for animals. This book covers the essentials of using essential oils safely and effectively to enhance your pet's physical and emotional health. From easing stress and anxiety to providing relief from pain and inflammation, each chapter is dedicated to a specific aspect of your pet's well-being.

Learn how to select the right essential oils, understand their benefits for skin care, respiratory health, and digestive comfort, and explore how aromatherapy can support aging pets or those with

---

1. https://books2read.com/u/bOEM69

2. https://books2read.com/u/bOEM69

separation anxiety. Discover natural solutions for flea and tick management, coat care, and even how to use aromatherapy in training and socialization. With a focus on safety and the importance of a balanced approach, this book is an invaluable resource for creating a harmonious environment for your beloved companion.

Also by Gonzalo Estrada

Self Healing
Visualiza tu Éxito
Cultivando Líderes
Afirmaciones y Empoderamiento
Semillas de Cambio
Cómo convertir TikTok en una máquina de hacer dinero
Cómo hacer dinero con Pinterest
Cómo hacer un ensayo
Cómo Pedir un Aumento de Sueldo
Currículo Poderoso
Entrenamiento sin Violencia
Entrevista Laboral
Gana Dinero con X (Twitter)
Ganar Masa Muscular
Volver a Empezar; el arte de reinventarse
Analiza Resuelve Ejecuta
Aromatherapy, The natural path to your pet´s well being
Holistic Feeding
The ABC of Educating Your Pet
The Art of Cosmic Connection
The Art of Feng Shui applied to your Pets
From Scarcity to Abundance
The English Bulldog in The Family
The French Bulldog
Therapeutic Massages for Pets

Pets and Crystal Therapy
The Maltese Bichon

About the Author

Gonzalo Estrada es un autor prolífico y reconocido, cuyos libros abarcan temas que apasionan a la humanidad. Con una presencia destacada en los principales medios tanto físicos como en línea, Estrada ha dejado una marca significativa en la literatura contemporánea. Sus obras, de gran trascendencia en plataformas como Amazon, Barnes & Noble y muchas otras, reflejan su profundo conocimiento y pasión por los temas que aborda. Desde el poder transformador de la gratitud hasta la singular personalidad del Bulldog Francés, Estrada ha demostrado ser un escritor versátil y cautivador que ha sabido conectar con lectores de todas partes del mundo.